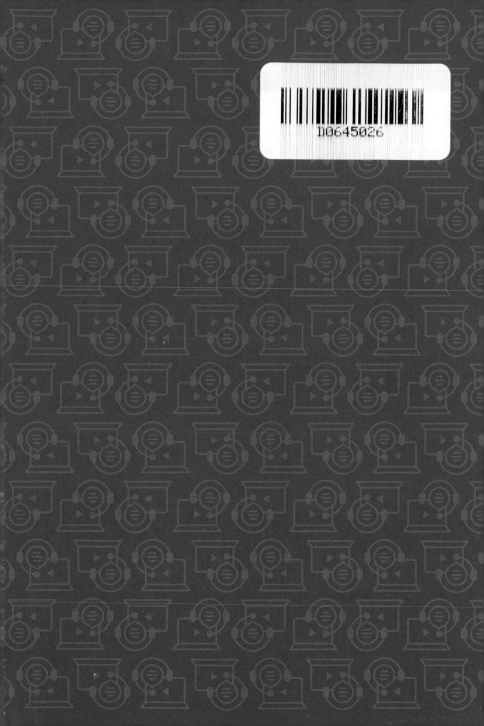

"Like having coffee with an expert"

BETTER PRESENTATIONS

How to Present Like a Pro (Virtually or in Person)

BY JACQUELINE FARRINGTON

IDEAPRESS
PUBLISHING

WASHINGTON, D.C.

IDEAPRESS
PUBLISHING

Ideapress Publishing | **www.ideapresspublishing.com**

Published in the United States by Ideapress Publishing.
All trademarks are the property of their respective companies.
Cover Design by Victoria Kim
Illustrations by Dan T. Walsh
Cataloging-in-Publication Data is on file with the Library of Congress.
ISBN: 978-1-64687-046-2

Special Sales
Ideapress Books are available at a special discount for bulk purchases for sales promotions and premiums, or for use in corporate training programs. Special editions, including personalized covers, a custom foreword, corporate imprints, and bonus content are also available.

Non-Obvious® is a registered trademark of the Influential Marketing Group.

1 2 3 4 5 6 7 8 9 10

DEDICATION

To all the brave souls who dare open their mouths
on stage or in front of a web camera

Read this book to learn how to imagine, create, and deliver captivating presentations in person or virtually by using the same proven techniques practiced by renowned actors, persuasive leaders, and popular TED speakers.

Is This Guide for You?

If you picked up this book, you are not a dummy.

Many business guides treat you like an idiot. Some even say so on the cover. This is not one of those books.

All **Non-Obvious Guides** focus on sharing advice that you haven't heard before. Lots of advice on speaking is either obvious (just breathe!) or cliché (imagine your audience naked!). In this valuable guide, Jacqueline uses her years of experience as a trained actor to break down exactly how to be more persuasive from the stage or over a webcam.

Using the same encouraging style that makes her such a popular speaking coach, Jacqueline breaks down the sometimes intimidating task of crafting and delivering a great talk into actionable steps with immediately useful advice along the way. You will be a more compelling speaker after reading this book.

ROHIT BHARGAVA
Founder, Non-Obvious Guides
2x TEDx Speaker + Keynote Speaker at 300+ Events

How to Read This Book

Throughout this book, you will find links to helpful guides and resources online.

FOR ONLINE RESOURCES, VISIT:
www.nonobvious.com/guides/betterpresentations

Referenced in the book, you will also see these symbols that refer to content that will further your learning.

FOLLOW THE ICONS

TEMPLATES
One-page templates to help explain concepts

DOWNLOADS
Excerpts or useful further reading

TUTORIALS
Detailed lessons on how to do a task

VIDEOS
Videos to watch online

CHAPTER SUMMARY
Key takeaways and important points

In this book, you will learn how to ...

- Start with strategic presence.

- Align your content, body language, and voice.

- Build inclusion with your audience.

- Rehearse with and without the equipment.

- Effortlessly present with other speakers.

- Make grooming, wardrobe, and background choices.

- Break away from expected presentation formulas.

- Handle the situation when everything goes wrong.

- Manage challenging, surprising, or annoying questions with finesse.

- Use expression in your voice to make your content come alive.

- Use improvisation to think on your feet.

Introduction

Public speaking can feel like a one-way form of communication, a simple transfer of information from the presenter to the audience. But speaking is actually a *two-way* interaction—and because the stakes are higher than just sitting around your dining room table after dinner with a glass of wine, it's an *elevated form of conversation*. **It's a performance.**

It requires engagement: inspiring a team to buy into a major organizational change, convincing potential funders to back your new business idea, shifting a company's diversity and inclusion efforts.

Whether a talk is delivered in person or in a virtual setting, the audience wants to be captivated, moved, inspired, persuaded, educated, and sometimes even challenged. And the best talks— such as Martin Luther King Jr.'s "I Have a Dream" speech or Franklin Roosevelt's fireside chats—spark emotion within us. That emotion imprints memories and ideas in our brains—and it changes our behavior, inspires us to action, and can even change the world. I learned this at a young age from a family story I heard many times growing up.

THE POWER OF ONE PERSON SPEAKING

My great-uncle Johnny was one of the 15 million Americans who were unemployed during the Great Depression. For years, he couldn't find a job, so he wrote a letter to then President Franklin Roosevelt asking for one.

FDR's fireside chats made Americans feel like they knew the president and he knew them. After each address, he'd receive millions of letters from people who felt personally connected to him. (Coincidentally, soon after sending the letter, my uncle had a job offer.)

Such superb speeches don't come easily. While Roosevelt's fireside chats *felt* informal, he prepared intensely. After spending *weeks* writing, trying out his content on staff and family members, he took one to three days to practice his radio delivery. Great presentations take work . . . and that's even more true today in a digital time.

Some people believe presenting virtually takes less work than delivering a live experience, so they prepare less seriously or maybe try to wing it. But presenting virtually or in a hybrid setting takes just as much, if not more, work, including many hours of experimenting with your words and aligning your tone and body language with your message, all to engage your audience and reach the goals of your talk. And whether you are in person or virtual, being persuasive enough to capture anyone's attention seems to get harder every day. In other words, learning to present better has become an even more critical business skill to have.

A BIG SHIFT SPARKED BY A TINY VIRUS

When Covid-19 hit, I was grounded at home, working remotely. In the first several months of the pandemic, I witnessed virtual presentations that were disjointed, boring, headache-inducing, and exhausting. Two years into the pandemic, most weren't much better.

Presenting well is not a short-term challenge. Those who understand how technology can support or erode their ability to communicate will be the most successful. Technology can enhance communications or make our jobs as communicators even harder. To succeed in the new world of remote, hybrid, or in-person work, leaders must fully embrace not just tools and technology, but also the techniques that make it work. We cannot forget that many of the skills required to present effectively online also are critical when trying to be persuasive in front of an audience. And they are exactly the skills that actors have been taught for decades.

WHY YOU NEED TO THINK LIKE AN ACTOR

Over the past 20 years, I've helped hundreds of speakers prepare for and deliver more engaging *performances*. I've trained actors for the rigorous demands of performing on stage and film, but I've also worked with a scientist speaking to an FDA advisory board meeting, a Big Tech CEO presenting to an audience of 20,000, a bank CRO discussing the economic implications of the pandemic with the International Monetary Fund, and many others.

My background in acting allows me to leverage acting techniques to help clients create **presentational performances** that are more dynamic, engaging, *human,* and authentic. Whether you're playing

King Lear or addressing the United Nations, you are delivering a *performance*. And a performance requires an elevated commitment of body, voice, mind, and emotions. A strong performance demands the speaker to be fully present and ready to adapt and respond to anything that happens in the moment.

In this book, you'll get a clear road map to effectively presenting with a performance mindset—no matter your industry, skill level, or audience. You'll save time, errors, and headaches, and learn how to meet the challenges of virtual presentations.

HOW GIVING BIRTH IN A DINER WILL HELP YOU, TOO

When I graduated as a classically trained actress with my MFA and started my life as a professional actress in New York City, one of my first auditions was for a TV soap opera. My MFA was focused on theater acting; in fact, I had taken zero camera acting classes. After the audition, the casting director, Betty, called my agent and asked me to come back in the next day, but to plan on staying for a couple of hours.

At the meeting, Betty said, "I think you're MAH-vuh-les. You have talent but you clearly have never acted for a camera before." She then spent the next two hours teaching me how to act for a television camera instead of a live audience. I went on to get the part. It was my first professional acting role, and my first scene was giving birth on the floor of a diner.

My hope is that this book will do for you what Betty did for me: help you deliver a more compelling performance no matter whether you are on a stage, in a boardroom, or in your home office in front of a web camera.

PART ONE

Preparation

CHAPTER 1

Presence

In the 2002 Winter Olympics, 16-year-old figure skater Sarah Hughes was in fourth place, and most experts expected her to stay there. "She should feel proud," said newscaster and former gold medalist Dorothy Hamill. "She can come back in another four years and be in a good position to win the gold." Favored to win that year was the reigning queen of women's figure skating, Michelle Kwan.

Hughes was the first to skate. She was perfect. As she ended her program, the audience was over the top—thunderous applause, cheering, shouting, a standing ovation. She won almost perfect scores from all the judges.

As Kwan took the ice, she was still favored to win the gold. But she stumbled and then fell. Then, came the contender favored for silver. She also stumbled. No other skater could match Hughes' performance.

Hughes became the youngest gold medalist in figure-skating history. In a memorable post-event interview, she shared what went through her mind before she took the ice: "Tonight I just said, 'I have nothing to lose.' I wanted to go out there and have a good time and skate for pure enjoyment."

Before she skated her performance of a lifetime, she wasn't thinking, "Be perfect." She *was* perfect because she focused on what she *wanted* to create and not on what she did *not* want to create. This allowed her to be fully present in her performance.

There are many definitions of *presence*, but while presence is about being noticed, it's not simply about drawing people to you. Through years of working with hundreds of speakers and leaders, I've discovered that you can have charisma without presence. You can be thrilling, interesting, and beautiful, and not be present.

Presence, at its core, is about the energy and connection that are shared between the performer and audience. This energy gives you vitality of physicality, breath, voice, mind, and heart. Being fully attuned to what you are doing, while being open to cues from the audience or environment, and possessing the agility to adapt to those cues in the moment—*that* is presence.

1.1   The Three C's of Presence

Based on years of working on presence with clients, I have developed three core foundations that help speakers build and maintain presence.

FOUNDATION 1   CONFIDENCE

Confidence is the ability to behave confidently even if you feel sick to your stomach with nervousness. It's also about building the mindsets, thoughts, and behaviors that support a confident delivery. Being confident doesn't mean never making a mistake. It does mean you have the ability to respond and adapt to anything that occurs in the moment.

FOUNDATION 2   CONVICTION

You can speak with conviction when you connect to your purpose for speaking and your purpose is connected to your audience. It also means aligning your reason for speaking to your values so you can stand in the power of your own conviction, knowing you are there to give a gift to your audience. Knowing this gift, your message, is bigger than your own fears gives you the conviction to speak.

FOUNDATION 3   CONNECTION

Connection means you show up for your audience with empathy and emotional intelligence. Nonjudgmental listening and a curious mindset also help you connect with your audience. In virtual presentations, it's important to use technology to connect with your audience, not to alienate them.

Each of these components relies on mindsets and other tools to build and maintain presence in all situations, with all audiences, and with any content.

THE VALUE OF POSITIVE SELF-TALK

Tessa worked for a well-known Japanese carmaker. As a high-potential leader, she was asked to present more often—and dreaded it every time. She grew so nervous during presentations that she'd forget her words, look down at the floor, or look at her notes. Then her voice would get so soft that people had to repeatedly ask her to speak up. She took a hard look at her thoughts and mindset. And discovered she was telling herself, "Don't screw up. They're watching you. If you mess up, your career is over." Talk about pressure! So, she committed to adjusting her self-talk: "Mistakes are normal. If I make a mistake, I have a plan for how to deal with it. The audience doesn't know my script, but I do." She also made a list of everything that could go wrong—and how she'd respond. She even worked on a pre-performance warm-up routine for her body, voice, and mind, so she was fully ready when she started. Finally, she reminded herself of her intention—the purpose behind her words, and the gifts in her message. Connecting to this intention and conviction generated more focus, and the fear lessened over time. While she still gets nervous, Tessa's come to understand the big-picture value of seeing how her presentations make a difference at the company—and in her career.

1.2	How to Develop Your Confidence

The first step in better presentations is building your confidence. It can also feel like the hardest thing to know how to do. Researchers in cognitive behavioral therapy have identified the cycle that leads to our behavior and outcomes. When a situation arises, the cycle of thoughts, feelings, actions, and results works like this:

1. **Thoughts:** We have thoughts and beliefs about the situation.

2. **Feelings:** The thoughts and beliefs trigger emotions in our brains.

3. **Actions:** Those emotions move us to act.

4. **Results:** Our actions impact the outcome of the situation.

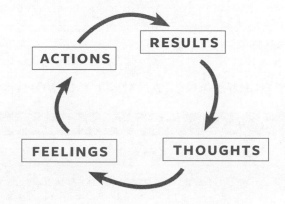

Thoughts lead to feelings, which lead to actions, which lead to results in how we show up.

Here's an example: I see something long and red in the grass. How I react will be based entirely on what I think it is. If I think it's a poisonous red snake, I'll feel fear and run away. If I think it's a piece of red string, I'll feel curiosity and investigate. If I think it's trash, I'll feel anger and might hurl a few expletives at the jerk who left it there, as I dump it in the garbage can. What we think leads to how we feel, which leads to what we do. So, to better control our outcomes, we need to better control our thoughts.

Let's apply this to a professional context. Say I am preparing for my first big presentation in a new role. The stakes are high. I know it will be a skeptical crowd and a make-or-break moment for my professional reputation. As I prepare for the meeting, my thoughts are already influencing the outcome. If I'm anxious, my thoughts may look something like this:

THE PERFORMANCE ANXIETY THOUGHT CYCLE

THOUGHTS	FEELINGS	ACTIONS
"I hope I don't screw this up. I am not confident and I know I'm going to screw up."	Fear	• Shaky, breathy, or high-pitched voice • Overtalking, rambling without pauses
"I always talk too much when people challenge me with questions. And given I'll be nervous, I'll talk too much. Don't talk too much!"	Doubt	• Hesitant speaking • Using lots of filler words like *um, uh, y'know*

THOUGHTS	FEELINGS	ACTIONS
"I'm nervous as hell about this sales presentation. This is my one and only chance to get it right. I have to do this right. I *have* to."	Pressure	• Pushing too hard to "make people get" the content • Not asking enough questions about the audience's needs
"This is virtual. I've never done virtual before. I hate virtual. I cannot believe I have to do this virtually. This is not my strength. What is it with these people that they're making me do this virtually?!"	Anger	• Talking over people, interrupting them • Using abrupt speech
"I'm not as prepared as I should be. I am sure they will ask me something I don't know how to answer."	Anxiety	• Reading solely from a script • Not engaging with the audience or adapting to their needs • Sounding like a robot

Our *thoughts* lead to our *actions*. To create the kinds of *results* we want, we need to behave or act in ways that lead to the outcomes we need. This means we need to *feel* the way that makes us *behave* that way. And in order to feel that way, we need to *think* that way. Here's how you might shift your thoughts:

THE PEAK PERFORMANCE THOUGHT CYCLE

THOUGHTS	FEELINGS	ACTIONS
"I will most likely make some mistakes, but that's okay. It will make me look human to the audience."	Reassured	• Remaining calm and focused
"Challenges from the audience mean opportunities to engage in a conversation. They're not out to get me; they want to explore the ideas."	Engaging and open to dialogue with the audience	• Asking clarifying questions • Remaining succinct, kind, and respectful when challenged • Smiling when someone challenges me, using open body language
"I've never done virtual before. This is a good opportunity to learn a new skill. I don't have to be perfect but I'll learn a lot."	Optimistic, hopeful, empowered	• Keeping a sense of humor if things go wrong • Remembering to breathe • Staying calm under pressure • Perhaps building a connection with the audience and their challenges at being virtual

THOUGHTS	FEELINGS	ACTIONS
"This feels like nerves. I'm feeling this way because this is important to me. I am excited and there's no difference in my body between excitement and nerves—other than how I view it in my mind."	Focused energy and excitement	• Being present, in the moment • Being able to check and adapt to the audience • Channeling the adrenaline into making your performance pop with focused energy
"I may not be as prepared for this as I'd like but I know this stuff. And I don't have to know EVERYTHING. Also, I can say 'I don't know' with calm confidence and then tell them I'll get back to them."	Empowered	• Being in charge, able to direct the audience's attention to important content • Being able to handle rough questions without getting flustered • Being able to admit "I don't know but I'll find out and get back to you" without appearing flustered
"I am prepared for mistakes. I have a plan. While I can't anticipate everything that might go wrong, even planning for some mistakes will help me better manage things in the moment."	In control	• Breathing and finding a solution when a mistake happens

These thoughts lead us to feel more empowered, optimistic, hopeful, and excited in the presentation, which means chances are strong that we will show up calm, adaptable, warm, and present.

> To build confidence, focus on what you *want* to create instead of what you *don't want* to create.

ACTING "AS IF"

When Anthony Hopkins created his chilling role as Dr. Hannibal Lecter in *The Silence of the Lambs,* he said he played the doctor as if he were a combination of Katharine Hepburn, Truman Capote, and the robot HAL from 2001: *A Space Odyssey.* Using the "as if" acting technique can help you feel and behave the way you want to (and need to) in any situation:

→   Think of a time when you felt wildly or solidly confident. Get specific. How many details can you remember? What did you say? How did you act? What was your body language like? How did you stand? Walk? How did your voice feel and sound? How did you interact with other people? They with you?

→   Now, do your presentation *as if* you are back in that time. Keep your content the same—don't change the words— but do it as if you are that wildly confident. Do it as the you from the past.

→ Another way to use this tool: Choose an extremely confident speaker. It can be Barack Obama, your boss, or your mom. It doesn't matter. Do the presentation *as if* you are that person.

VISIT ONLINE RESOURCES FOR:
Ideas and tips for how to use an "as if" and different "as if's" you can try.

1.3 How to Demonstrate Conviction When Presenting

Conviction is belief—in what you're saying, in your purpose for being here, and in the values that brought you here, now, today.

> Standing in your conviction allows you to deliver your content with confidence and connection.

Here are four tips on how to tap into your conviction:

TIP 1   ALIGN WITH YOUR VALUES

Find what in your content resonates with your personal values. Why does it matter to you? Why is it important to you? Spend some time reflecting on your content and how it aligns with your beliefs.

TIP 2   AIM FOR HELPFUL, NOT GOOD

I'm not even sure what a good presentation looks like. But I do know that when I aim to be good, amazing, or enthralling, I usually end up overacting. Changing our mindset to "My aim is to be helpful" puts the focus on the audience and off ourselves. It's nearly impossible to be present with an audience if your focus is on "being good." We end up either pushing content on them or making ourselves nervous by obsessing about results. Focusing on how we can add value, give a gift, or help people, changes the focus from being good to being of service.

TIP 3   CONNECT WITH A BIGGER PURPOSE

Why is this message important for the *audience*?

> When we connect with a purpose greater than ourselves, we forget our own petty worries and fears.

It's not about *me*; it's about the message, and we are just a vehicle to deliver it.

TIP 4   REMEMBER THE GIFT

What is the gift you are bringing to the audience today? If you are not present—if you are distracted with your notes or feeling defensive because someone challenges you—it will be difficult to give them your gift.

FEATURE:
THE TOP THREE PRESENCE KILLERS

- **Pushing too much out:** Being so focused on transmitting an idea to the audience that you overact and build a relationship that's pushing ideas on the audience. It creates the feeling of "You NEED to get this!"

- **Focusing too much in:** Being laser-focused on yourself and how you are performing. This sounds like a voice in your head saying, "I'm so nervous. I'm going to look stupid."

- **Forcing things to go exactly as you planned:** Being unable to adjust in the moment to new information from the environment or audience. The voice in your head says, "I must get through this content today, come hell or high water."

1.4 How to Build Audience Connection

Connection is the two-way street that you build with your audience. These tips can help you use connection to create presence:

TIP 1 PRACTICE LISTENING

Build in moments where you check in with your audience (use a poll or simply ask a question). Summarize and paraphrase what you've heard (not verbatim) to confirm you picked up the underlying values and emotions. Show that you understand what matters to your listeners.

TIP 2 GET TO KNOW THE AUDIENCE

Learn as much about your audience as you can before your presentation: What are their expectations, concerns, cultural preferences, and likes/dislikes?

TIP 3 PRACTICE AWARENESS

Sit in a café and observe others around you. What do you notice? Close your eyes and observe your breath for a minute. This starts to train your brain to notice when you mentally check out and stop paying attention to others.

TIP 4   READ LITERARY NOVELS

Reading about others' lives helps you build the muscle of empathy—the ability to walk in other people's shoes.

TIP 5   PLAY WITH IMPROV

Improv helps keep you present in the here and now. It helps you think on your feet and respond authentically to others.

Note: For more on building audience connection, see Chapter 7.

1.5	**Choose How You Show Up: Presence versus Strategic Presence**

Strategic presence is the ability to adjust how you show up in different situations in order to meet your audience's needs and help them hear the message. It's particularly important in virtual presentations where energy is harder to read. Here are some examples of changing your presence to fit the audience, situation, and content.

IF YOUR NATURAL PRESENCE IS	SITUATION AND OBJECTIVE	YOUR STRATEGIC PRESENCE
Driver: takes the lead in suggesting solutions, takes charge, and has no problem being at the front of the room	Listening tour to inform a new role; encouraging other people to share ideas	• The Introvert • Asking questions, waiting for answers • Pausing, allowing silence • Sitting with the team or even in the back of the room
Judger: is quick to evaluate or critique the merits of ideas and outcomes	Brainstorming session	• The Connector • Withholding evaluations and offering ideas • Letting others talk first • Not being the primary speaker
Detailer: is focused on not missing a thing—crosses every "t" and dots every "i"	Selling an idea	• The Visionary • Using vision, big-picture inspirational language • Delivering with emotion • Moving the audience from one emotional state to another
Reflector: loves to listen, lets others talk; asks for opinions or seeks consensus before acting	Subject matter expert presentation	• The Visionary Driver • Laying out your vision for the plan • Sharing your research and advising next steps

You might be thinking after reading this chart that it feels like manipulation. Isn't this acting? Lying? Covering? Being inauthentic? Absolutely not. Just like how a person has many roles (e.g., leader, mother, friend), there are many ways to be present. As humans, we are wonderfully equipped to dial up or down different aspects of ourselves in order to fill the need of the moment.

STORY:
CONFIDENCE IN BOTH SELF—AND OTHERS

An émigré to the United States from India, Rajeev went from an impoverished childhood to running a successful business on Wall Street. His tough, hard-driving business acumen helped him become a wildly successful CEO. His remarkable ideas of running a business led to media profiles and to guest slots on talk shows. Until one day they didn't.

Attempting to command and control, Rajeev didn't listen to colleagues. He talked over people and ignored their contributions. His firm was losing clients to new, disruptive competitors who poached his employees.

He was killing ideas and innovation. And when I shared this feedback with him, he looked like he might throttle me! But he heard it.

It's impossible for someone to fully rid themselves of their "old" presence, but we focused on expanding his repertoire. Rather than command from the front, Rajeev started sitting silently in the back. He asked others to set the agenda. He listened to colleagues' questions—and brought more curiosity to hearing the answers.

Over time, many of his teams' ideas were implemented. The company started wooing back previous clients—and winning new ones. He didn't lose his tough street smarts. But he learned to share the journey with others. His staff now describe him as a forceful but fair leader—with the confidence to let others sit in the driver's seat.

VISIT ONLINE RESOURCES FOR:
An exercise on how to build strategic presence.

CHAPTER SUMMARY
KEY TAKEAWAYS:

- Presence is created through confidence, conviction, and connection.

- Our mindset is a powerful tool or detractor when it comes to building and maintaining presence.

- Strategic presence is making intentional choices about how you show up for your audience, the situation, and your content.

CHAPTER 2

Setting the Scene

In any presentation, there are moments that *feel* like a close-up. In virtual or hybrid presentations, nearly *every second* is a close-up. There's a lot of eye-time focused on your head, your shoulders, and the smartly decorated shelves in the background. The audience is evaluating everything in that tiny video frame, either consciously or unconsciously.

Think about how you watch others present. By the end of an hour-long presentation, you have examined every visual detail, from the pattern in the speaker's scarf to the slightly open door behind them. As an audience member, you are constantly scanning for information that will help you better understand the presenter's message, and everything you see is a colorful little piece of that puzzle.

Your decisions about your clothing, grooming, and background (or, should we say costume, makeup, and set design) all contribute to how the audience processes your presentation. If you want them to be successful listeners, you need to help them focus—with your words and your appearance. In other words, you need to set the scene.

2.1   Choosing the Right Clothing

When it comes to your presentation wardrobe, you don't have to be a fashion maven. You do need to make a few strategic choices to ensure you pop into your audience's minds. What you wear validates your role, so push the Tommy Bahama shirt to the side for now and reach for clothes that bring out your best. Here are three tips that will help:

TIP 1   WEAR WHAT MAKES YOU FEEL COMFORTABLE

You'll be more confident if you're not distracted by a fit, color, or pattern that's just not you. Be sure to avoid anything you'll be tempted to fidget with. Put on your chosen outfit well in advance of your presentation and record yourself in a rehearsal while wearing it. Feeling it and watching the playback will help you know that you'll be comfortable and confident.

TIP 2   WEAR WHAT'S APPROPRIATE FOR YOUR MESSAGE

Your audience will factor your clothes into their overall impression of you. Will you be received as a meticulous expert, charismatic creative, or tech-savvy consultant? If you go for softer, less structured clothes, make sure they don't look lumpy or disheveled because that can undermine your authority.

The moment when Allen realized the video conference had not yet ended.

TIP 3 WEAR WHAT LOOKS BEST ON CAMERA OR ON THE STAGE

Think of how the colors, textures, and lines of your clothing contrast against your background. On stage or virtual, make sure to wear a color that contrasts with your background. Wearing black on black can make you look like a floating head. The camera or stage lighting doesn't always see things the same way your mirror does, so give your wardrobe a screen test or ask a friend for feedback. Does your shirt make them dizzy? Is that orange shirt hard on the retinas? Does your gray sweater and gray background make you look like a disembodied head?

The bottom line is, you are the show, not your clothes. You need to be focused on your content, not that suit jacket that feels hot, the hosiery that's itchy, or the tie that's choking you. If comfort to you means yoga pants during a virtual presentation, no judgment. Just be aware that being underdressed can make you feel uncomfortable, too, especially when it could undermine your message.

A client of mine is the CEO for a large tech firm, and he always wears the same thing. It's the look made iconic by Steve Jobs—jeans, dark shirt, no tie—the uniform of mavericks. Wearing it tells people, "I'm putting my mental energy into something bigger than my closet."

Having a go-to outfit means you know yourself. It can also help lessen the stress of last-minute preparation because you have one less detail to think about.

No matter what you choose to wear, just remember to be strategic. What you wear gives your audience context about your personality and the tone of your presentation.

 VISIT ONLINE RESOURCES FOR:
A framework for choosing what to wear.

2.2 Makeup (Not Just for Women)

As with clothing, makeup should make you feel your most confident and comfortable. That means if you're not normally a bright-red-lipstick-and-eyelash-extensions person, the day of your presentation is not the time to try it out.

Stick to what feels the most *you*, and *stay* close to reality with just a little extra polish. You want to look like the most vibrant version of yourself—not a caricature.

EIGHT TIPS FOR A GREAT FACE

If you wear makeup, read this entire list. At a bare minimum, tips 1, 5, and 7 are important, even for people who don't wear any makeup. If you're not a regular user of makeup, using it well can make a big difference to how you appear on stage or camera:

TIP 1   FEAR THE SHINING

A shiny, oily face will make you look sweaty and nervous (which makes your audience nervous, too). Use a blotting sheet to quickly soak up excess oil. If you're confident with makeup, apply a transparent mattifying cream or translucent loose powder to your forehead, nose, and chin—and keep the application light.

TIP 2   EVEN OUT THE TONE

Color correctors hide imperfections by cancelling out unflattering hues with opposite shades. This means they can tame the red flush of a killer hangover or dark circles from sleep deprivation. Apply a bit of green to camouflage redness, purple to neutralize yellow spots, or orange to take care of dark circles.

TIP 3   ADD DIMENSION

Webcams can dull color, turning your face into one flat circle devoid of natural highlights and contour. To bring out your cheekbones, apply a light gel blush in warm tones like coral or peach. Avoid blue tones like pink as they'll look darker on camera.

TIP 4   DEFINE YOUR EYES

Eyebrows are your exclamation points. They add structure and expression to the entire face. If you want your eyebrows to pop, fill them in with a powder color. This will give you a much more natural look than pencils. Use eyeliner to frame your eyes with a very thin line close to the lashes.

TIP 5   WAKE UP

To erase dark circles under your eyes, apply a concealer, but remember to blend, blend, blend. Another trick to look more alert is to add highlighter at the inner corners of your eyes and curl your eyelashes.

TIP 6   KEEP COLOR NATURAL

Shadows from your camera setup can quickly darken out your eyes. If you wear eyeshadow, choose a neutral color that's one to three shades lighter than your skin tone.

TIP 7   MATCH TO SKIN TONE

If you wear foundation, make sure it matches your natural color. Go to a makeup counter and ask several makeup artists to recommend one that looks right for you. Always check the foundation outside in natural light, and ask for a sample you can try at home. Apply foundation in natural light and blend it down into your neck for a consistent look.

TIP 8   WET YOUR WHISTLE

Keep your lips moisturized with lip balm, but avoid lip gloss. The sticky texture of lip gloss can make you want to lick your lips, which looks very Hannibal Lecter. Opt for nude lip pencils and soft, natural-colored lipsticks to add definition.

2.3   Improving Your Background (for Virtual Presentations)

We've all been on video calls where participants made odd background choices. You try to focus on their words, but find yourself wondering why their bed has so many embroidered pillows. Whether it's a bookcase stacked with business canon or a blank brick wall, your background tells a story, so choose it carefully. In short, dress your background with the same care you put into your wardrobe. The first step is to reconsider your virtual background.

Just because you *can* add a virtual background, doesn't mean you *should*.

One Harvard study[1] found that audiences prefer seeing speakers in their real environments and rated them higher for trustworthiness, innovation, and expertise. The study also found that virtual screens, and even blank walls undermine a speaker's gravitas and authenticity. You don't need a Harvard study to know that no one wants to see you making a professional presentation in front of a random beach scene or looking like you're in the cockpit of the Millennium Falcon (unless you're presenting about Star Wars, of course).

In the world of virtual, people love to see the real you.

Of course, there's a risk in sharing too much of you. Nobody wants to see your dirty laundry (literally), or get a peek into your en suite. So, before you decide on the perfect spot to set up your camera, make sure the background is camera ready. Here are tips to make it work:

TIP 1   CLEAN IT UP

Wash the dishes, make the bed, remove all the messy papers lying around. You are inviting your audience into your home or office. They appreciate it being warm and personal, but it should also be tidy.

TIP 2   PROP IT UP

Audiences love to see insight into your personal style—with books, framed pictures, plants, or flowers, and even furniture choices that reflect your interests and taste.

TIP 3   GIVE IT DEPTH

Include as much of the room behind you as you can. Proprioception is how we determine our spatial relationships to things around us (more on this in Chapter 7). When speakers use fake backgrounds, our proprioception gets thrown out of whack, increasing fatigue.

TIP 4   SKIP THE FAKE NYC SKYLINE

Fake screens don't give you any points for authenticity. A stock image of the mountains is beautiful, but it just makes the audience wonder, "What is this person hiding?" Green screens also have the added ick factor of green-screen spill, which can make your audience wonder if they're high on something. Green screens are fine within a professional studio setting, but avoid them when presenting from home.

"Is he moving in front of a green screen,
or is that the weed we smoked kicking in?"

TIP 5   PAPER IT UP

If you can't find an uncluttered, non-distracting space to present from, a quick workaround is to tape seamless photo paper on the space behind you. (It doesn't have to be white.) It won't give you the personal look audiences prefer, but it will at least prevent them from seeing your dirty dishes.

TIP 6   COMPARE YOUR ROOM

Check out the folks at Room Rater on Twitter @ratemyskyperoom. This couple started rating the rooms of politicians and celebrities during the pandemic and now have hundreds of thousands of followers. You may not agree with all their ratings, but you can find some cool ideas here.

CHAPTER SUMMARY
KEY TAKEAWAYS:

- In virtual presentations, you are always in a close-up. Take care to make sure everything within your frame looks its best.

- Be strategic about your grooming and wardrobe choices. Make choices that feel comfortable, fit the situation, and support your message.

- Think about how your face, hair, clothes, and background work together. Are they complementing or competing?

CHAPTER 3

Congruency

Ever asked someone how they're doing and then doubted their answer—but couldn't quite put a finger on why? Maybe you asked an associate how a meeting went. While they replied, "It went well," your instincts told you otherwise. It wasn't the words, but how they were delivered that felt off. Saying "well" while behaving "not well"—that's incongruency in communication.

Whether you're talking to your boss or ordering a cheeseburger, every communication is actually two conversations at once:

Conversation 1: The actual words you're saying

Conversation 2: The vocal and nonverbal communication: your tone of voice, rate of speaking, emphasis, facial expressions, gestures, posture, and position in the room relative to other people

When both of these conversations are aligned, our listener hears and understands us. We are being congruent. We are more credible. But if the two conversations are sending out different messages, our listener believes the second conversation—every time.

To send clear messages to our audience, we have to be intentional—not accidental—in how we use our body, voice, and words.

EXERCISE:
OBSERVE BOTH CONVERSATIONS

The next time you're talking to someone, notice the "second conversation" they're having with you. Notice their body language and pay attention to what you find inspiring or compelling, confusing or contrary. How are their words supported or undermined by their vocal and nonverbal communication?

3.1 | How to Read and Use Nonverbal Cues

Ever notice that you gesture when talking on the phone, even when the other person can't see you? That's because we're programmed to use gestures to help convey meaning.

Scientists hypothesize that we rely so much on the unsaid because understanding physical cues used to keep us alive. Early humans used nonverbal communication long before we had words to determine whether the other person's intent was to help or hurt us.

We use all of our senses to quickly determine whether someone is a friend or foe. We quickly scan for meaning beneath words. We pay attention to tone and volume of voice, rhythm and pace of speaking, words emphasized, enunciation, gestures, facial expressions, proximity, and posture.

> We read eye contact, stance, and gestures to determine status, decide who can be trusted, and recognize the difference between ally and enemy.

Today, our brains are still highly attuned to listening and watching for signals first. Our minds are deeply encoded to evaluate what people do over what they say. And we're constantly monitoring and re-evaluating their behaviors based on minute adjustments they make.

EIGHT COMMON TYPES OF NONVERBAL CUES

CUES	EXAMPLES
Facial expressions	Smiling, frowning, brows knitted together, or wide eyes (angry, happy, sad, disgust, surprise)
Eye contact	Looking directly at each person or not making eye contact; making fleeting/flitting eye contact or holding eye contact too long (hello, serial murderer)
Gestures	Nodding or giving a thumbs-up (we can gesture with our head too, something Abraham Lincoln was noted for)
Posture	How you sit or stand—open or closed, angled toward or away?
Proprioception	Our spatial relationship to things and people around us; the sense that tells us where our body is in space
Autonomic reactions	Automatic responses such as rapid breathing or sweating
Touch	Physical contact with the audience such as handshakes and hugs

3.2 Why Reading Nonverbal Cues Is So Hard

In virtual communications, our ability to process cues and behavior is greatly diminished because the signals we rely on are muffled by technology. The camera shrinks and flattens us.

Eye contact is actually camera contact. And most of the time, all we have to look at is a huge talking head with little stick fingers that pop in and out of the frame. Even our voices are significantly distorted. In fact, here are some common incongruencies that affect both in-person and virtual presentations:

→ **Not making eye contact:** Telling people, we're "so thrilled to see them" as we glance away.

→ **Fidgeting:** While annoying on stage, small movements are magnified in virtual. For example, rocking back and forth in our chair can read: I'm bored and ready to move on or I'm extremely uncomfortable.

→ **Monotone voice:** We *say* we're excited about something, but we *sound* bored to tears.

→ **Hesitant speech:** We insist we're confident, but we say *um* or *y'know* every five words.

→ **Distracted by our notes:** We tell people we want to connect with them, but look like we're reading off a teleprompter, confidence monitor, or second screen.

→ **Shadowed faces:** When our lighting only reveals part of our face, our expressions are difficult to interrupt.

→ **Over-gesturing:** Do we want our audience to look at us— or at our hands?

→ **Under-gesturing:** When we don't show our hands at all, we appear to have something to hide.

3.3	What Message Are Your Nonverbal Cues Sending?

We tend to think about someone's gestures only when they're alarming or out of sync with what the person is saying. But we constantly decode subtle messages through voice and body language.

Our vocal patterns and nonverbal communications signal directly what we're feeling, thinking, and intending. Without knowing it, our actions can tell people to ignore our words.

WHAT ARE YOU TELLING PEOPLE?

VERBAL MESSAGE	NONVERBAL CUE	POSSIBLE MESSAGE RECEIVED
We can do that.	Averted eye contact	I have no idea if we can do that.

VERBAL MESSAGE	NONVERBAL CUE	POSSIBLE MESSAGE RECEIVED
Let's get started!	Leaning back in chair	I don't want to be here.
I'm excited to be here today.	Eyes darting back and forth between notes and the camera	I have no idea what I'm doing or I'm so nervous I could cry.
This strategy is bold and will ensure our success.	Inserting lots of *ums* and *uhs*	I don't believe in this strategy.
Everything is fine.	Clenching jaw or speaking through gritted teeth	I'm pissed as hell.
Everything is under control or I'm calm.	Hands fluttering rapidly in and out of frame. Feet "dancing" around the stage, or shifting from foot to foot.	I'm a wreck. I'm an emotional mess. I'm scared to death.
This matters to me.	Shrugging shoulders	I couldn't care less.
Please feel free to be yourself.	Swatting your kids away and giving them scathing looks when they come into the room	I'm not okay being myself.
I believe in this product.	Playing with hair. Fidgeting with a pen.	No, I don't.

VERBAL MESSAGE	NONVERBAL CUE	POSSIBLE MESSAGE RECEIVED
I love connecting with people.	Not showing my video	No I don't.
I want to be here.	Slouching, leaning head into hand on desk	I'm tired.
Tell me more.	Nodding	I agree with you.
This strategy is bold and will ensure our success.	Looking directly at the camera	Let's do this!

VISIT ONLINE RESOURCES FOR:
A downloadable guide on how to practice your congruency.

STORY:
THE MONKEY AND THE PEANUT

A study done in the 1990s monitored the brain activity of monkeys to see how they responded to eating peanuts, a favorite food. The study showed that every time a monkey ate a peanut, the pleasure centers of their brain were activated.[2]

One day, a researcher in the lab popped a peanut into his mouth, and the monkey's pleasure center lit up as if she had eaten the peanut herself. From this, researchers discovered that humans and monkeys have "mirror neurons" that mimic the actions and emotions of those around us.

When we see someone experience joy or sadness, our mirror neurons light up and we experience it with them.

Let's say you tell a group, "This is exciting stuff," but sound bored. Your audience's mirror neurons will tell them to feel bored with you. If you say, "I'm so excited to be here today," but actually look and sound anxious, they will feel anxious with you. This is why congruency matters.

We need those mirror neurons to understand each other. But in virtual, we lose much of the opportunity to activate them because we can't fully see or hear a person. With this limited information, congruency between your words and actions is even more critical in amplifying the feelings you want your audience to experience.

CHAPTER SUMMARY
KEY TAKEAWAYS:

- People's brains are trained to trust visual signals, so the words we say must align with the actions we *show* to be believable.

- Be aware of how nonverbal cues like gestures and facial expressions can affect your audience—they feel what you feel.

- Make intentional choices about your nonverbal communication to support the tone and meaning you want to convey.

CHAPTER 4

Rehearsal

We never witness all the hard work that Meryl Streep invests in her craft. We don't see the five hours of daily practice Itzhak Perlman puts into playing his violin. We don't see the endless pliés and tendus that ballerina Misty Copeland does as part of her daily routine. But because they deliberately practice, day in and day out, they *enthrall* us.

Instead of making you appear robotic or canned, rehearsal frees you up to enjoy your presentation.

The performance becomes not just a part of your brain's memory, it becomes part of your body's memory, too. Yet rehearsing a presentation isn't the same thing as *memorizing* it. Paradoxically, rehearsing helps ensure you appear *un*rehearsed.

...5,347...
5,348...
5,349...
5,350...

The Bolshoi Ballet's star ballerina on her day off

> Great presenters deliver content like it's flowing fresh from their brain. They look relaxed and natural and *unrehearsed* because they have practiced over and over and over and over again.

So how can you learn to rehearse like a pro?

4.1 Why Rehearsing Matters

Rehearsal can feel like a daunting task—and it's probably because you never learned *how* to do it. But first, let's explore *why* it matters so much.

→ **Frees your brain to communicate, not just recite.** When you are so prepared that you're not thinking about what comes next, your next line or slide, you can concentrate on the most important thing—your audience.

→ **Makes you adaptable in the moment.** A well-rehearsed presentation means you can respond to your audience's needs by cutting content, jumping ahead to different sections, or rewinding to clarify topics. To do that, you need to free your brain.

→ **Prepares your brain for the worst.** Sound cutting out, internet going down, audience can't see your slides— we can never anticipate every curveball , but when we practice, our brains are primed to more easily manage the unexpected. The playwright Samuel Beckett said: "Fail, fail, fail better." If we accept that something is likely going to go wrong, rehearsal gives us more opportunities to discover it, deal with it, and make it go *right*.

→ **Helps manage performance anxiety.** When we don't rehearse, we risk jumping into our presentation and experiencing the "weird factor" for the first time: "Why does my voice sound like that? Whoa . . . this silence from the audience in a virtual presentation is weird."

Repetitive exposure—doing it again and again and again— reduces the anxiety that often precedes a big event.

When someone hasn't rehearsed, you can tell. They stumble, use a lot of fillers, and their body language isn't connected to the meaning or emotion of their speech. Why? Because their brains are distracted by the novelty and anxiety of the moment. And when they're distracted, so is their audience.

→ **Makes you more creative.** Some of the most creative moments happen in rehearsals because you're trying things out.

In rehearsal, without the pressure of perfection, it's okay to see what works and what doesn't.

Your discoveries lead to inspirations about: "Oh THIS would work!" Stand-up comics are known for testing new material in clubs and then tweaking it based on the audiences' responses. Rehearsal gives you options so you can be better in the moment. The worst time to try to be creative about what you are going to say is when you are saying it, with all eyes on you.

→ **Gives you a sense of timing**. Rehearsal helps refine your content. You can time yourself and see where you're running long or short. Are there chapters of your presentation that are long-winded and risk losing the audience's attention span? Which areas beg for more time engaging with your audience? When you know your presentation backward and forward, you have the power to make it better.

In my years of coaching speakers to take the TEDx stage, we never rehearse on the stage on which speakers will ultimately deliver their talks. But we do give each speaker the opportunity to at least *walk* on that same stage to get a feel for it. That first moment a speaker walks onto their performance stage is telling. Seeing that stage and those 3,000 empty seats is a wake-up call. The speakers who *haven't* rehearsed get spooked. The ones who *have* put in the footwork might have a gulp moment, but they quickly recover and remind themselves that they've prepped.

4.2 How to Mentally Rehearse

It's hard to not think about something once it's in your head. Here's what top athletes and their coaches know: For every physical and fundamental act, there is an equally important and equally related mental component that must be addressed. Instead of telling herself *not* to strike out, or *not* to make an error, the player thinks about what she *wants* to happen. For example, an athlete might think, "My eye is on the ball" instead of "Don't lose sight of the ball." In presenting, this means trading in "I am not prepared" with something like "I am focused."

STORY:
I'M NERVOUS

A few years ago, I was sitting on a stage about to speak to a group of 500. As the host for the event was getting ready to introduce me, I noticed my hands were shaking. Then I noticed my breath was shallow and speeding up. "Oh my god," I thought, "I'm NERVOUS." And then I went off into a whole inner monologue, "How can I be nervous? I'm never nervous. I teach this stuff. I can't be nervous. Stop it."

Guess what? As I sat there telling myself, "Don't be nervous," I grew even MORE nervous! And I started to feel sick to my stomach. Given I was standing on stage, I had to recover quickly. So, I switched to telling myself, "I'm excited. I'm thrilled to be sitting on this stage about to speak. I'm excited. I'm going to connect with a great group of people. I want to be here." All of my emotions were SCREAMING, "No, you are NOT excited. You are nervous. You're going to bomb." And I kept catching myself and changing my self-talk to, "Excited, I am excited to be here. Excited to share this with the audience."

My heart rate began to slow down. My breathing evened out. After a minute, I felt calmer and after another minute I was focused and clear—just like I told myself I was.

Here are a few tips for mastering the art of mental rehearsals:

TIP 1   THE LIST

Make a list of every thought you have around your upcoming talk. Once you've got a list of 10–20 thoughts, divide them into two columns: 1) Thoughts that will help me and 2) Thoughts that may not help me. The goal is to keep your attention on the thoughts that help.

TIP 2   SNAP IT BACK

Put a rubber band on your wrist. That's your reminder to manage your self-talk. Every time you catch yourself focusing on what you DON'T want to create (e.g., "Don't rush this part"), snap that rubber band and choose a new thought ("Take your time here"). Have a list of new thoughts memorized so you don't have to search for one in the moment.

TIP 3   CHECK IN WITH YOUR BODY

The next time you feel physically nervous—shaking hands, heart pounding, dry mouth, tense shoulders or neck, sick to your stomach—stop and ask yourself, "What am I thinking right now?" Because we experience emotions physically before we are cognitively aware of them, it's important to check in with yourself to understand what's happening and identify the thoughts that are creating this physiological response.

TIP 4   FLIP THE NEGATIVE

Sports coaches know a powerful tool to transform mistakes: thinking positively *immediately* after an error. They train their players that chastising themselves after a mistake only risks making the same mistake again. By thinking positively about the event, "I'm glad that went wrong—now I know how to deal with it," they replace the fear of making another mistake with the empowerment of learning.

| 4.3 | **Should You Memorize Your Presentation?** |

I personally don't like memorizing. It puts your focus on repeating the exact words, rather than communicating and connecting with your audience.

Instead, I often teach speakers how to *remember* a talk without memorizing. Here are five tips that work:

TIP 1   USE NOTES

The first few times you're rehearsing, go ahead and use notes—use them as many times as you need. Then, as you grow more confident with the material, start lessening your use of notes. A page becomes a paragraph, a paragraph becomes one to two sentences, one to two sentences become two to three words; then one word; then, finally, an image. Eventually you create a storyboard of images that take you from point to point. (Hint: these might be the same images as on your slides.)

TIP 2   INTERNALIZE, DON'T MEMORIZE

Know where you want each section of your presentation to land, the take-home message, but give yourself wiggle room on how you arrive there. Instead of speaking it exactly the same every time, know your topic so well that how you get to your main point can change.

> Internalizing your talk is like driving home. You know the route so well, you can take any turn you want and still arrive at the same house.

An easy way to do this is to break your talk into sections.

TIP 3 MEMORIZE THE IMPORTANT STUFF

> Be sure to fully memorize your introduction and your conclusion. Start strong and end strong.

If you start strong, the audience will forgive a multitude of sins. Also, memorizing the beginning will carry you through any nerves you have at the top.

Additionally, focus your memory power on what you absolutely cannot get wrong: data points, facts, quotes.

TIP 4 REHEARSE IN A "MEMORY PALACE"

If you've never seen Anthony Metivier's wonderful TED Talk on memory palaces—it's worth a watch. One key takeaway: Go through your "memory palace" taking different routes. If you always enter from the front door (the beginning of your talk) and then head to the coat closet, rehearse entering your palace through the back door, then head to the bedroom.

> Run through your presentation forward, backward, and out of order. Make it bulletproof so you could jump into any spot and easily find your way back into the talk.

TIP 5   FLY WITHOUT INSTRUMENTS

Aka running through your presentation without notes or a script. Yes, this one is painful. It will make you want to hit someone. Just do it. Do it a few times. Do not stop, no matter how awful it feels. If you stumble, force yourself to recover and keep going so that you get through the talk in real time, several times before you give it. Ask a friend to be on-book for you (meaning they hold the script). Every time you forget a line, stay focused—don't break your concentration—and simply say, "line." Your friend then reads a few words to jog your memory, and you pick it up from there. This is great for identifying sections where you need more time and work. It also helps you fully own your material.

| To practice effectively, you need to be mentally, physically, and technically prepared.

| 4.4 | **Eight Rehearsal Habits of Great Presenters** |

HABIT 1 PHYSICAL REHEARSAL

If baseball players only rehearsed by throwing a pitch or hitting a ball in their *heads*, they'd be booed off the field. So, while taming your mental state is crucial, you need to rehearse physically, too.

The main difference between mental and physical rehearsal is that in physical rehearsal, you're making noise. It includes:

→ Speaking out loud, the way you will on the day of your talk

→ Connecting to and showing the emotion of your talk

→ Using gestures (even if small)

→ Handling props, if used

→ Using your slides

→ Rehearsing in the space or as close to the space you'll be speaking in

HABIT 2   BREAK OUT THE BEAT

Actors divide their scripts into beats—which is simply a unit of thought—but you can think of it as any time you have a change in emotion, a new thought, a new tactic, or a new engagement tool. You can give your script chapters titles like this:

→   Chapter 1/Beat 1: The memory

→   Chapter 2/Beat 2: From memory to discovery

→   Chapter 3/Beat 3: What this discovery meant

Once you've divided your talk into chapters, you can rehearse them one at a time. This makes rehearsals more manageable and a little less intimidating. I often catch my husband and give him a quick rendition of one chapter with, "Hey, what do you think about this?" Bam! I've rehearsed!

HABIT 3   GO FOR GRADUAL

Remember rehearsal isn't about perfection; it's about trying out your material, playing with your delivery style, and building on your mistakes. Even if you walk away from a rehearsal having figured out a better way to deliver just one sentence, you've moved forward.

Set the goal of improving your delivery just a tiny bit each time you rehearse and making one new discovery about your presentation.

HABIT 4   REHEARSE ALL OVER THE PLACE

Rehearse while doing the dishes, taking a shower, going for a walk, moving on the elliptical trainer. Rehearsing doesn't mean you need to always stand and deliver as you will on the day. You can and should rehearse whenever, wherever possible. So if you find yourself doing something that's not mentally taxing, take the opportunity to run through a portion of your presentation.

HABIT 5   WATCH YOURSELF REHEARSE, BUT NOT IN A MIRROR

Seeing how you present is valuable in determining what works and what doesn't. But rehearsing in front of a mirror can make you super self-conscious and self-focused. Using a mirror can get you accustomed to watching yourself as you speak, and that's a temptation you definitely want to avoid in virtual presentations. Besides, your audience will be able to tell.

Instead, video record yourself. Then acting as if you're watching a total stranger, jot down:

→   What does this person do that works?

→   What could they do better?

→   What should they try next time?

HABIT 6   GET FEEDBACK FROM A SMART, IGNORANT AUDIENCE

Speaking to a real person reminds you that humans do exist on the other side of the camera and creates the reality of in-person communication in your brain. Be sure to find people who know nothing about your topic. They will tell you if they're confused or lost. With services like virtualorator.com, you can rehearse in front of a live audience. If you can afford this, it's a useful rehearsal tool for rehearsing with complete strangers and getting honest, constructive feedback.

HABIT 7   CREATE SOME STRESS FOR YOURSELF

Ask friends or family members to throw challenging or irrelevant questions at you. Or ask someone to call a member of your audience during your rehearsal, so you have to deal with distractions. Rehearse while blasting out the volume on music you absolutely can't stand. Remember, going over your talk in your head will not replicate the same stress as showtime, so try to create some pressurized situations to build up your stress tolerance.

STORY:
AUDIENCES FROM HELL

In a "Presence and Presentation" course my team and I delivered for a global bank and a pharmaceutical company, we created "audiences from hell." Their phones ring. They get into side conversations or even arguments with each other. They text, type on laptops, and generally do their best to be terrible listeners.

Putting the speakers through their worst nightmare makes them feel like the real deal is a cakewalk.

HABIT 8 GIVE YOURSELF TIME TO PLAY

It's easy to get stuck in the belief that when you rehearse, the objective is perfection. It's not.

> Rehearsal is about trying techniques to make discoveries about what works.

The only way those discoveries happen is through experiment and play. Try these ideas:

→ **Italian run.** This is an old chestnut from theater. When a cast gets stale in their delivery, a director orders an "Italian run." Here, the actors go through the entire play, saying and doing everything twice as fast as normal. The beats are still there, and they don't skip words; they just do it fast. This breathes new life into the delivery and gives you confidence that you know your stuff. If you stumble, just keep going!

→ **Overact it.** In addition to breathing expression into your voice, when you overact, you'll discover new emotional highs and lows that will inspire how you deliver the final presentation.

→ **Underact it.** Now, take all the emotion and expression out of your delivery. Just go through the content by rote. You'll discover that you need and want the emotion back in—and that there's more emotion than you realized.

4.5 Mastering the Technical Rehearsal

You're probably familiar with the panic that happens when technology breaks down at a live presentation. The adapter's wrong, the videos won't play, or a mic cuts out. When you're in the same room as your audience, you can wing it. In virtual, without your tech, the whole experience is compromised. So if you're presenting virtually, make sure you practice at least three times with all your technology, at least one week before going live.

Technical checklist for virtual presentations:

→ **Hardware:** Computer, camera, mic, speakers, lighting

→ **Software:** Video platform, chats, polls, settings

→ **Internet:** Speed and bandwidth

→ **Backup and redundancy:** What's your plan if something breaks? For example: have a "Back Soon" slide ready to go up in case of technical issues.

VISIT ONLINE RESOURCES FOR:
For a "Before Take-off Technical Checklist for Virtual Presentations."

TEST IT WITH AN AUDIENCE

The best way to get comfortable with technology in virtual presentations is to use it. Invite people to your virtual rehearsal to give you feedback on sound, lighting, camera angles, and what you're wearing. If you're using a producer, make sure they join you to test out every tool. Knowing your tech and being prepared with backup scenarios are critical (but often overlooked) parts of delivering a stress-free, seamless virtual presentation.

> Say to yourself, "F**k it."
> Whatever happens, happens. If you can do this, you will soar.

STORY:
F**K IT

The best advice on rehearsal that anyone ever gave me was from a college professor. He told me, "Rehearse until you're sick of rehearsing. But then, when it comes to performance time, put that work you've done in your back pocket. Know it's there and it will serve you. Then, forget about it. Say to yourself, F**k it. Whatever happens, happens."

CHAPTER SUMMARY
KEY TAKEAWAYS:

- Rehearsal doesn't make your presentation stiff; it sets you free to be in the moment.

- Rehearse both mentally and physically so that your mind and body are ready to go on game day.

- Know your talk inside and out, forward, backward, and sideways.

- Rehearse in front of a friend or practice audience to get valuable feedback.

PART TWO

Delivery

CHAPTER 5

Voice

It's a cruel betrayal when a highly intelligent person is sabotaged by the sound of their own voice. Speaking too quietly, too fast, too slow, too anxiously. Experts, leaders in their fields, people whose ideas can change the world—the value of their content can quickly be diminished because their voices are hesitant, meek, or irritating.

I once worked with a law student who decided to run for public office. He was a delight—warm, smart, engaging. He had two challenges, though: He'd never held nor run for public office, and when he spoke, he sounded like a robot. All the expression left his voice, and he sounded as if he was rattling off instructions for assembling an IKEA shelf. But after a year of working on his voice and body language, he beat the incumbent to win his race.

Even the most interesting people discussing fascinating topics can sound like they're bored to tears. I call this "slinging content" at people. It's like a having your server at a restaurant sling your dinner plate onto the table—and walk away.

Our voices tell the audience so much through volume, pitch, pacing, and articulation. With just the tool of our voices, we're able to implicitly signal what is cool, fascinating, or important.

5.1   Why Do I Sound So Weird with a Mic?

In the same way virtual presentations shrink and distort our image on camera, much of the sound spectrum of our voice is missing when we speak with a microphone.

Microphones compress our vocal overtones and undertones, making our voices sound small and "tinny."

Additionally, in virtual presentations, an internal computer mic picks up many distracting ambient sounds such as fingers typing.

How can we compensate? One way is to buy a good mic. The best solution, though, is to develop a voice that is alive and expressive.

Your audience wants to hear what you have to say—all of it. By intentionally engaging key voice attributes, you can compensate for much of what's lost between microphone and speaker.

TO BE HEARD, USE YOUR EARS

E = Energy (volume and speed)

A = Articulation (consonants, vowels, and the words you choose to emphasize)

R = Resonance (the quality of your voice, including pitch and tone)

S = Stops (allowing for pauses and avoiding fillers)

EXERCISE:
LISTEN TO YOURSELF

The best way to know how others hear you is to record yourself and listen. Yeah, it's painful—our head voice sounds different. But until we learn how we actually sound, we won't know what could be improved.

Use the voice memo feature on your phone to record yourself explaining what you ate for breakfast, describing a project you're excited about, or leaving a message for a colleague. Then, listen to your voice a few times before assessing it:

- What adjectives describe my voice?
- How do I think others would describe it?
- How would I want it to sound different?

If you don't like your voice, change it. Just like when you exercise your muscles at a gym and they get stronger, the human voice is also made up of muscle and cartilage, which means you can develop it through regular exercise. If you don't like the way your voice sounds to others, you can add warmth, range, and rhythm.

Think about what you heard when you listened to yourself. Which EARS area is your greatest opportunity for improvement? Let's take a deeper look at each of these four elements.

VISIT ONLINE RESOURCES FOR:
A listening guide to audit and improve your voice.

5.2   How to Improve Your Vocal Energy

Different presentations require different kinds of energy. If you're trying to rally an audience into action, you'll want to exude excitement. If you're trying to get them to think deeply and compassionately, you'll want to sound calm and caring. Whatever tone you want to set, two of the biggest contributors to energy level are speed and volume.

There is not one, optimal tempo for speaking.

> In general, a good rate of speech ranges between 110 to 160 words per minute.

When we're nervous, we might hit 200 words per minute, which can make us impossible to comprehend, especially for global audiences.

Even when our speed is well moderated, mix up the pacing to surprise the listener and match the speed to the content. The *contrast* you create between rhythms—leaving that baseline—will wake up your listener.

> Faster speaking is often associated with humor and lighter messages. And slower speaking with complex, serious, or more important content.

VISIT ONLINE RESOURCES FOR:
A sample of different speaking speeds and a guide for how to practice your pacing.

Volume is the second way to add energy and drama to your content. We tend to use loud volumes to demand attention and softer volumes to pull people into us to listen. Again, with volume, it's all about the contrasts. For example: You might say, "Our profits this year are through the ROOF." Then, "But it's our *spending* [*quiet voice*] that is out of control." Here are some tips on how to use volume specifically to impact your vocal energy:

TIP 1   SPEAK QUIETLY FOR SUSPENSE/ENGAGEMENT

Speaking quietly can signal to the audience to lean in. We often use a softer volume when speaking confidentially or emotionally or to build suspense.

TIP 2   RAISE THE VOLUME

Raising the volume can indicate something that's celebrated or contested.

TIP 3   MASTER THE STAGE WHISPER

Use a stage whisper to capture attention. A stage whisper is a whisper that's intended to be heard. The voice is gone but the speaker uses energy and animation in articulation. For example, imagine whispering to your partner in a restaurant to *"Stop. IT!"* when you want your partner, and not the entire room, to hear and pay attention to you. When using a stage whisper, make sure to hit the final consonants of words and lengthen the vowels to make the words pop.

TIP 4   USE THE ELEMENT OF SURPRISE

Surprising changes in volume can be funny or attention-grabbing. They can shock a listener (think of the "whispering aside" convention in which the speaker includes the listener in a private joke that the other people on stage are clueless about).

5.3 Using Articulation Like a Professional

Articulation is how we use the sounds in our words. For example, if I say, "Shut up," I can say it without hitting the consonants very hard: "shuddup." Or I can hit the consonants hard: "Shu**T** u**P**." For American English speakers, the meaning changes drastically from, "You've got to be kidding" to "Stop talking immediately." How we articulate different words tells listeners how to interpret our tone.

Similar to articulation, word emphasis affects meaning by telling the listener which part of the sentence is most important. For example: The **boy** ran to the store. The boy **ran** to the store. The boy ran to the **store.** Notice how the emphasis changes the meaning.

> Use your voice like a highlighter to help listeners remember what's important.

When all our words sound similar, the audience doesn't know which ones to pay attention to, and the even rhythm can lull them into boredom. By emphasizing words and articulating word parts, your voice makes the content more "scannable" for key points.

VISIT ONLINE RESOURCES FOR:
Tips to practice articulation.

5.4 Understanding Resonance, Projection, and Vocal Pitch

Resonance is what gives your voice its color and timbre. It is also key to projection and volume. Are you frequently told it's hard to hear you? Don't work on "speaking louder." Work on resonance—"speaking fuller." A resonant voice is full and rich, that "syrup over pancakes" quality that news anchors and actors are known for. But remember, your voice is air and muscle. If it isn't naturally resonant, you can change it.

To do that, it helps to understand a bit about anatomy: when you speak, air moves from your lungs and passes through your vocal folds. The sound this makes is amplified when the air in your throat, mouth, nasal passages, and chest vibrates sympathetically with the air passing through your vocal folds. Without that amplification, the human voice is barely perceptible.

If you close down your airstream with tension in your neck, throat, tongue, soft palate, and shoulders, only a small part of the sound spectrum is amplified. Loosen and open up those areas, and your voice sounds richer and *louder*. One way to do this is to speak with what actors call "pre-laughter."

To achieve pre-laughter, the sense you want in your throat is as if you are about to laugh, or yawn. Imagine someone has given you a surprise gift, and when you open the box, you take a tiny breath of delight as you exclaim "Oh wow, thank you!" This begins to give you a sense of openness in your throat, mouth, neck, and jaw.

Your optimum pitch is where you're most resonant.

Optimum pitch is the note around which our voice is the clearest, most efficient, and most resonant. Learning to use optimum pitch in professional speaking is one of the best things you can do for vocal expressivity and health. Want to practice your optimum pitch or learn more about how to develop a more resonant and fuller voice? There are many exercises that actors learn for doing exactly these things. I have compiled the best for you in the online resources section of this book so be sure to use them!

Years of trying to lower her voice
resulted in significant vocal chord damage.

STORY:
EVEN OPERA SINGERS NEED VOCAL COACHING

I once worked with an opera singer with a magnificent singing voice—a soprano who regularly performed onstage at the New York's Metropolitan Opera. Her speaking voice, though, was the issue. For years, she'd been told she sounded like a little girl when she spoke. And if she wanted to be taken seriously, she should speak with a lower voice. While she practiced good vocal health when singing, her efforts to push her speaking voice down to a lower pitch caused unnecessary tension, pressure, strain, and—ultimately—damage. So together, we focused on how she could speak with greater resonance and support. Once she did that, she spoke with a more powerful voice—without hurting herself.

VISIT ONLINE RESOURCES FOR:
Useful vocal exercises to build your resonance, practice your pitch, and improve your voice overall.

5.5   What Are Hellers and Why They Can Destroy Your Presentation

When we think about presenting better, we often focus on the words, and not the spaces between words. But these stops have great value in our ability to interpret and retain information. When used intentionally, stops give a speaker a chance to listen, to signal the importance of a statement, and to let their audience process. But when stops are cluttered with *hellers* (fillers) they're no longer elegant pacing tools. Let's start with the bad kind first.

"So, umm, I just want to talk with you about yesterday? Y'know, December 7th, 1941, a date which will basically live y'know like live in, ummm, infamy, right?"

Recognize the speech? Imagine if President Roosevelt had addressed the nation this way as the United States entered World War II.

Instead, this quote is one that we still remember today, over 80 years later.

"December 7, 1941. A date which will live in infamy."

Roosevelt delivered his message with conviction, passion, and credibility. He used language that was clear, immediate, and direct. If he delivered it full of hellers, the quote itself would not still be remembered so many years later.

WHAT THE HECK ARE HELLERS?

Hellers is a term I coined that describes the combination of hedges (*I just, I kind of, basically, sorta, actually*), fillers (*um, like, y'know, uhhhhh*), and qualifiers (turning statements into questions). Hellers cause our communication to lack conviction, credibility, and engagement. They also make us incredibly hard to follow.

HELLER EXAMPLES

WHAT YOU MEAN	HOW IT COMES OUT
This is the right choice.	This is the right choice, *right?*
We should move forward.	We should probably move forward.
Her work is world-class.	I think her work is world-class.
Our core values are inclusion, collaboration, and integrity.	Our core values are, um, y'know inclusion, collaboration, and, like um, integrity.

When we're not 100 percent comfortable, hellers let us keep talking without the pressure of saying something concrete.

HELLERS DESTROY CONFIDENCE

Hellers prevent our audience from hearing, trusting, and engaging with our content. They signal we're not quite certain about our message. And, with hedges (*I think, I feel, I just want to, I kinda, sorta, maybe, possibly, actually*), they tell others that what I'm about to say isn't really what I believe.

> Use language that is clear, direct, and immediate.

FOUR TIPS FOR ELIMINATING HELLERS

TIP 1   ASK FOR HELP LISTENING

Most of us are not even aware we use hellers. Ask a friend or colleague to be your "um buddy" and point out your hellers. Have them ask you a question about your opinion on a complex topic. As you respond, they can gently clap, touch your shoulder, or hold up their hand each time you use a filler, hedge, or qualifier. Have them keep a list of hellers, so you can reflect on them when you practice alone.

TIP 2   STOP, BREATHE, REPEAT

When your "um buddy" points out your heller, take immediate action to redirect your behavior. Stop, breathe, and repeat what you were saying immediately before the heller, only this time without it. Stopping helps us become intentional. Breathing helps us stay focused. Repeating helps us retrain the mind and body.

TIP 3   KNOW WHEN YOU'RE DONE

Using upspeak (turning statements into questions) or adding words like "yeah?" and "right?" at the end of a sentence, signal that you're not sure about what you're saying. While practicing your presentation, remind yourself to stop at the end of a thought: throw a ball against the wall, kick a box, or hit the table on the last one to two words of each sentence. The physical action is a temporary substitute for the unnecessary filler, just until you get used to stopping naturally.

TIP 4   USE AN APP

Ummo is a great tool that lets you track your progress on eliminating hellers, by detecting when you use filler words like *um*.

STORY:
YOU WANT TO BE A LEADER, RIGHT?

Joe was a top-performing director, already in charge of a large team, at JPMorgan Chase. He had the chops and experience to move to the next level, and was on deck for a promotion. But he was told he lacked the gravitas to be seen as a next-level leader. Something was holding him back. But what? I asked if I could observe him in action. Turns out, he ended nearly every phrase or sentence with "right?" "We need to revise this report, right? It's not what the client needs, right?" In just one five-minute meeting, I counted over 100 "rights," and gave up counting. While this heller wasn't the only thing holding him back, he was inadvertently asking for permission on *everything* he said.

5.6   Stops and the Power of Pausing

Pauses can give you more gravitas and confidence. The most powerful communicators pause, sometimes for extended periods of time, to allow their messages to land. These speakers are not rushed, nor do they feel the need to fill silence with a heller or repeat what they just said. A pause in speaking can be the length of a half breath, or even several seconds.

> ### STORY:
> ### DID YOU KNOW? PAUSES ARE CULTURAL
>
> ---
>
> As you present, keep in mind how different audiences use pauses. Linguist Deborah Tannen found that people from New York use fewer and shorter pauses than people from Los Angeles.[3] And Yuka Shigemitsu at Tokyo Polytechnic University found that while Americans often fill the gaps during conversations, Chinese and Japanese speakers don't mind long pauses at all.[4]
>
> Whether you're comparing regional or global cultural differences, it pays to listen to your audience and mirror their rhythm to increase their comfort and open the door to a stronger connection.

Using pauses effectively means you're letting silence do the heavy lifting.

Let the audience consider the idea for a moment. Or wonder about the question. It can make you look more thoughtful as you consider what you want to say next. It can build suspense and drama. Here are three secrets that actors know about using effective pausing to create an effect:

TIP 1   CREATE BOOKENDS

If you've got something big and juicy to say, stop speaking just before the idea, and then a little longer immediately after you've said it.

TIP 2   GIVE SPACE FOR ANSWERS

If you ask a question, stop. Even if it's a rhetorical question. Even if you don't expect people to answer, allow time for them to consider a response in their own heads.

TIP 3   GET COMFORTABLE WITH SILENCE

If you forget what you're saying, don't add an *um*. Just pause and breathe. Breathing will fire up your brain to help you remember your next thought. Filling the space with empty words that add no new value will only distract your audience.

STORY:
TWO CANDIDATES, ONE WINNER

In the 1992 presidential debate between President George H. W. Bush and Senator Bill Clinton, Bush was clearly prepared for the moment. Each time the moderator asked him a question, he immediately jumped in with his response. In contrast, nearly every time Bill Clinton answered a question, he paused and took a few seconds to consider his response. Most pundits agreed: President Bush seemed on the defensive, while Clinton appeared commanding, comfortable, and thoughtful. His pauses were interpreted as confidence. He won the debate, and went on to win the election.

CHAPTER SUMMARY
KEY TAKEAWAYS:

- The quality of your voice contributes to your believability and engagement as a speaker.

- Exercising your voice can help improve your energy, articulation, resonance, and stops.

- Knowing how to use silence—and avoid hellers—can add drama and emotion to your talk.

CHAPTER 6

Body Language

To communicate with congruency, you need your body to be on its best behavior. Body language is a powerful indicator of emotion, intent, and meaning that people with high empathy are accustomed to watching and interpreting.

FBI interrogators use body language to uncover intent in life-or-death situations. Though your understanding of body language may not feel like it carries quite so high stakes, understanding these nonverbal cues can often mean the difference between connecting with an audience and falling flat.

Body language includes eye contact, gestures, posture, spatial relationships, and facial expressions. Any one of them can be a ruthless saboteur to your content.

6.1 Get That Body to Behave

Body language is a very powerful ally when used intentionally. Thanks to mirror neurons, when people see a speaker whose mind and body are in sync, they feel in sync, too.

> Nonverbal communication helps our audiences understand *what* we're saying and how they *feel* about our message.

When our body language contradicts our words, our audiences can become confused, distracted, and anxious. Ever find yourself watching the hands of an animated speaker instead of listening to his words? It doesn't matter what he says if you're wondering, "What's going on with those hands?"

TEN NEGATIVE BODY LANGUAGE SIGNALS TO AVOID

1. Dancing distractedly back and forth or slouching in your chair

2. Darting your eyes from notes, to participants, to chat function, to off camera, to the floor

3. Over-gesturing with an action for every single word

4. Cutting off gestures by not bringing them fully into the frame of a camera

5. Not using any gestures at all

6. Watching your own video on a virtual call

7. Erupting with sudden or explosive gestures that aren't tied to what you're saying

8. Squinting or leaning over to see people

9. Touching your face or playing with your hair

10. Playing with pens or shuffling papers

EXERCISE:
BODY LANGUAGE AUDIT

Before trying to change your body language, first understand how you use it now. Record yourself giving your presentation, and download the questionnaire to audit your use of expressions, eye contact, gestures, posture, and stance. This exercise will help you be more strategic about your choices in frequency, intensity, and style of your gestures.

VISIT ONLINE RESOURCES FOR:
The Body Language Audit.

6.2   Ten Tips to Create Eye Contact in Virtual Presentations

While eye contact can be difficult in person, in the virtual meeting world, it's even harder. When we look at our audience, we end up looking at an image of them, which takes our eyes away from the camera. So, from their perspective, we're looking away.

Bottom line: The main focus of your eyes needs to be looking into the camera. But unlike trained actors, most people are uncomfortable looking into the eye of a camera.

Here are 10 tips on where and how to focus when you can't see your audience:

TIP 1   LOOK HERE

Add a sticky note next to your camera that says "Look here." Remind yourself that your audience is right behind that lens or beyond that little bright dot.

TIP 2   SEE A FRIENDLY FACE

Place a picture of your greatest fan right next to your camera. It can be your partner, best friend, or even your mom. Every time you look into that camera, you'll see their picture, and it will remind you that you are speaking to real human beings.

TIP 3   DON'T STARE

Treat eye contact much like you do in real life. This means briefly looking at your notes, at the chat function, or at your participants. If you stare at the camera, you'll look like a serial murderer. Try to hold eye contact for around five to seven seconds before looking away.

TIP 4   MAKE KEY POINTS TO THE CAMERA

Identify the key ideas you need to land with the audience. Make sure your eye contact lands on the camera at those key points. When you glance at your notes, always read ahead so you have a chunk of content you're delivering without looking at your notes. This takes practice!

TIP 5   BREAK WHEN YOU BREATHE

The best time to break eye contact is at the end of a phrase or sentence, when you breathe. Try this: Finish a phrase or sentence; then take a breath. On the breath, take a moment to glance at your notes to see what's coming next.

TIP 6   TAKE SEVEN-SECOND PAUSES

When you ask a question, look at the participants for about seven seconds before looking back at the camera. You can look back and forth as long as you hold your gaze at either the camera or the participants for about seven seconds.

TIP 7   MAKE YOUR EYES VISIBLE

If you wear glasses, wear antiglare lenses, so your eyes aren't lost in the reflection. If you're not directly speaking to a slide, don't get lazy. Take it off screenshare so the audience can see you.

> Your audience needs to see your eyes to connect with you, so make sure your face is the main event.

TIP 8   MAKE NOTES READABLE AT A GLANCE

Use a large font size for your notes so you can see them without squinting or having to lean in to your camera.

> It's okay and *natural* to break eye contact to look at your notes, the chat box, or your attendees.

We don't constantly hold eye contact in live meetings, so release yourself from the pressure of having to do it in virtual.

TIP 9   POSITION WINDOWS AT THE TOP

Move the video conference box and your notes to the top of the screen so they're close to the camera. This will direct your energy toward the camera. With smaller groups, I tend to move the screen of the person who's talking so it appears highest on the screen, right below the camera, so I'm looking in the right direction.

TIP 10   USE MORE THAN ONE MONITOR

To mimic the natural eye contact of an in-person presentation, I suggest using three monitors. The main monitor is for the camera and your notes. A second is to see the participants and chat. A third is to keep an eye on your slides. This setup creates less brain strain by separating tasks and making everything bigger. But it's crucial to rehearse this way. Don't wait for presentation day to try it.

 VISIT ONLINE RESOURCES FOR:
A downloadable template of the virtual setup that I currently use.

6.3   How to Use Gestures Effectively

When presenting in person, the wide-open space of a large stage can handle a lot of gestures.

On screen, not only is there less space—it's also more concentrated. That is, smaller things are amplified. Think of it by comparing a stage to a film screen. In a movie theater, an actor's face is about 8 feet high and 15 feet wide. A computer monitor has the same concentration, so every gesture packs extra punch. Here are some tips on how to use your body to tell the audience what's important:

TIP 1   GET IN FRAME AND STAY THERE

Make sure your audience can see at least the upper third of your body, so that your upper arms are in the frame. Make sure your whole hand is visible when you gesture. Avoid those little finger stick figures that happen when people only gesture in the bottom part of the frame.

TIP 2   CREATE A HOME POSITION

Imagine you are the center of a clock and your home position for your hands is 10:00 and 2:00. Your computer should be far enough away that your arms are slightly extended, but not so far that you lock your elbows. (I usually stand between two and two and a half feet away from my computer.) This will help fill up the frame a little more. It's also easier to gesture from a place of space rather than having your arms tight against your body.

TIP 3   DON'T BE AFRAID OF STILLNESS

Remind yourself to return to your home position and be still. Speakers who have moments of complete stillness accentuated by purposeful movement are perceived as more credible and trustworthy.

TIP 4   USE YOUR HANDS EARLY AND EFFECTIVELY

When we see another person's hands, our brains relax a little. That's because, at the subconscious level, we perceive empty hands to be non-threatening. Also, avoid gesturing toward the camera. It can make your hands look huge so they steal all the focus. Instead, try to focus closer to your body—around your chest and head—to keep everything in proportion.

TIP 5   MAKE YOUR GESTURES PURPOSEFUL

Notice if your gestures are attached to the meanings of your words, or are they repeated over and over without meaning? If it's not supporting a specific concept or emotion, don't do it.

TIP 6   KNOW WHERE YOUR SLIDES ARE

If you are presenting with visuals on screen, use gestures to point to what they can see. If you have a second monitor where you see your slides, move it so your audience perceives that you're looking at the same slides they are.

TIP 7   USE THE RULE OF THIRDS

The Rule of Thirds divides your screen into three horizontal sections:

1. **Upper third:** The eyes and above, leaving two to three finger lengths over your head

2. **Middle third:** The upper chest, neck, and face, up to your eyes

3. **Bottom third:** The chest to torso

STORY:
MOVING BEYOND A MEANDERING DISASTER

When I met Christina, she was a respected research scientist at a well-known pharmaceutical company. But after she gave a rather disastrous delivery during a high-stakes meeting, the CEO declared, "Do not let that woman near a presentation ever again!" Ouch. That's when Christina and I began working together.

First, I could see that she spoke her entire practice presentation . . . to the floor! Our bodies and our voices are always in tandem. So, with Christina's eyes at her feet, her voice landed there too, making her nearly impossible to understand. Further, she meandered all over the stage—which, you guessed it—caused her voice to "meander" too. Lacking focus, energy, and expression, Christina's hard-to-follow sentences were filled with hellers: "um," "uhhh," and "y'know."

We worked on more purposeful movement—with clear destinations each time she moved. Say, making eye contact with people on the right side of the room before she intentionally moved there. Finally, I coached her on posture and on finding moments of stillness. With her more confident body language, aligned with her voice, she moved more in tandem, and with a more commanding presence. She went on to become a leader at a top government health agency.

6.4 Why Posture Matters (Hint: It's Not Just for Preventing Back Pain)

To sit or to stand? The answer is: It depends. First, think about your strategic presence. How do you need to show up in this presentation to help your audience hear what you're saying? What does the space you are presenting in mean for the "right" posture to use? If you are presenting in an informal and friendly meeting room, standing may convey an overly aggressive posture. If, on the other hand, it's a formal setting, then choosing to sit may be seen as a sign of disrespect. Sitting and standing, in other words, must be an intentional choice.

SITTING

If you need to come across as more approachable and informal, sit.

When to sit:

→ If you want the session to be more conversational rather than focusing on you

→ If you are doing a longer presentation, where standing might be exhausting

→ If there's not much room to move around within the frame of the camera

Sitting tips:

→ Make sure both feet are firmly planted on the ground.

→ Don't sit back in your chair. Sit on the edge so you can sit up straight. This helps you support your voice and speak with energy and commitment.

→ Make sure you don't use a chair that can swivel. Swiveling back and forth in a chair is distracting and makes it hard for your audience to focus on what you're saying.

→ Put a pillow behind your lower back. This will remind you not to slump, which can make it seem like you're giving it a half effort.

STANDING

If you need to come across as formal and authoritative, stand.

When to stand:

→ If your presentation is an hour or less

→ If you want to recreate the feeling of an in-person presentation

→ If you are the main event and you want all eyes on you

Standing tips:

→ Have your feet at least hip distance apart to give yourself a solid base and prevent slouchy posture.

→ Keep your knees released, slightly bent, and bouncy. If you lock your knees out, the rest of your body will look stiff or unapproachable.

→ Record a practice session and watch out for slumping or "dancing feet." Too much back-and-forth movement is distracting.

Sitting or Standing: A Quick Posture Check-In

To avoid slumping, hunching, or standing too stiffly:

→ Imagine your spine is being pulled up from the crown of your head. The crown isn't the very top of your head. Rather, it's where you'd wear a skullcap if you were a priest—think the top back of your head.

→ Now imagine, at the same time, your spine is also being pulled down through your tailbone. It's like your spine is a rubber band, gently being pulled in two different directions simultaneously.

→ I like to put one hand on the crown of my head and one hand on my tailbone and think about my head growing into my hand while my tailbone is dropping down toward the floor.

→ Next, relax and drop your shoulders. Pull them up toward your ears, and then let them naturally drop down and away.

This is a great "mini-break" to do throughout the day. It helps you look and feel alert.

PASTURE POSTURE

EXERCISE:
WELCOME TO MY PARTY

Opening the front of the body: Another way you can avoid hunching is to imagine you're welcoming a big group of guests to your house for a celebration. You open your arms up and wide (almost like you're going to hug the group) as you say, "Welcome everyone, *Mangia, Mangia!*" Then, simply let your arms drop to your side while keeping your chest open and slightly lifted. You'll find you're more open through your shoulders and upper chest.

SPLITTING THE DIFFERENCE

If you have a longer presentation—maybe a workshop where you're speaking for part of the time and then collaborating with the group part of the time—you can move between sitting and standing. Stand when you need all focus on you; then switch to sitting when you want the audience to engage more.

CHAPTER SUMMARY
KEY TAKEAWAYS:

- Body language can completely change the meaning of your message. Use your body to bring more emotion and clarity to your words.

- Eye contact, gestures, facial expressions, and posture are just as important to your presentation as your verbal content.

- The decision whether to sit or stand is dictated by your strategic presence goals.

CHAPTER 7

Connection

Humans have a need to belong. We learned long ago that cooperating with one another was essential to our survival as a species. Those who were part of a group could more easily attack an enemy, find food, and reproduce. Being alone meant being another species' lunch.[5]

In too many presentations, it can be tempting to skip connection and get straight to the content. But failing to connect actually impedes your message. If people don't feel connected to you, they'll likely not listen at all.

So how can you build a powerful connection with your audience—whether you are there in person or presenting virtually?

7.1 Seven Ways to Create More Audience Connection

When we blast out information, we sometimes end up talking *at* our audience rather than *with* them. In person, the audiences' presence in the room can remind us to take a moment to receive their reactions to our words. Whether we're speaking virtually or in person, we need to be intentional about connecting to the conversation.

Here are some tips on how to do that:

TIP 1   WRITE CHECK-IN MOMENTS INTO YOUR SCRIPT

To remind yourself to stay away from the monologue, you can write things like "pause" or "group pulse check" into your notes.

> In virtual presentations, make sure you do some kind of engagement piece, at least every 10 minutes, to keep your audience with you.

TIP 2   PRACTICE TO A REAL PERSON

Try your introduction on the grocery store clerk. Ask your mom if you can give her your conclusion. Treat your husband to a romantic rendition of your first section, right before bed.

You'll see if they're nodding their heads, or if they're looking confused. Their feedback will alert you to where you may need a check-in for clarity with your actual audience. Do this as many times as you possibly can.

> When you present in front of a real person, you'll connect to the reality of speaking with a human being, and it will become muscle memory.

TIP 3 WARN THE AUDIENCE THE SESSION WILL BE INTERACTIVE

With virtual, people often expect they're going to get online and hear someone droning on. If you give them a heads-up that you will be asking them to participate, it helps them prepare and sets the expectation for engagement. Conversely, if they're not prepared to talk and are called on without notice, they may be embarrassed or even put off—and your goal is to create connection, not pain.

TIP:
LEADER HEADS-UP

When possible, ask the team or function lead to send an email to the audience participants about the participatory nature of your presentation. People are more likely to read an email from their leader and follow his or her instructions.

TIP 4   SEND THE QUESTIONS YOU'LL BE ASKING BEFORE THE SESSION

Explain that you'll be exploring the questions in the session and looking for responses. This step can also be a great conversation starter as participants are arriving at the beginning of your meeting.

> If you're going to ask questions that require some reflection, sharing them ahead of time will ensure your audience is prepared to contribute.

TIP 5   REMIND THE AUDIENCE TO SPEAK UP

Right at the beginning of your presentation, give your audience a nudge by reminding them that they'll be talking too. Here are a couple ways to frame it:

"We'll be pausing throughout today's presentation to hear some of your insights and perspectives."

"This is going to be interactive. I'll be asking some questions for us to explore together. Please be prepared to share your thoughts via chat or over your mic."

TIP 6   ASK EVERYONE TO TURN ON THEIR CAMERAS

> Eighty-two percent of virtual participants are less likely to multitask when their camera is on.

So, if you're doing a virtual presentation with an audience of 40 or fewer, ask to see their faces. This not only helps them focus, but it's also easier for you to see if they're tracking with you. It also creates more of a sense of being in the room with one another. Since they may not normally use their camera, be sure to tell them ahead of time so they can be presentable and not show up in their PJs.

Are you presenting in a hybrid situation? Make sure you are inclusive by asking everyone to join the meeting from their own room or cubicle. It's exclusionary when some gather together onsite in the same room and others call in from individual locations offsite. The folks in the room together will have more opportunities for communication and decision making or influencing. So, as much as possible, level the playing field by asking everyone to call in from a discrete location.

TIP 7   NEVER SACRIFICE CONNECTION FOR CONTENT

If you realize you're nearly out of time, but you've got half of your content left, cut the content. You could try to speak faster and cram as much as possible into your allotted time, but guaranteed, if they don't connect with you, they won't hear what you're saying. To be fully heard, you may need to say less.

HOW TO EXPRESS GRATITUDE

If you want your audience to contribute, make sure they are rewarded for it by showing them that you appreciate their involvement. You can do this through:

ACKNOWLEDGMENTS	Verbally recognizing the contribution	"Thank you for your input."
FEEDBACK	Commenting on, extending, or replaying a summary of someone's contribution	"That reminds me of what we discussed earlier." "So, what you are saying is . . ."
NONVERBAL CONFIRMATIONS	Sounds or gestures that confirm you are processing what they are saying	"Uh-huh," "ah, yes," and "mmmm," nodding your head

7.2   How to Use Feelings, Experiences, and Perspectives to Build Connection

To form a connection with any audience, you must be deliberate about bringing feelings into your presentations. Our own experiences and stories, as well as the different perspectives from people in the audience, can help create that emotional bridge between people. Here are some key ideas to use:

TIP 1   USE EMOTIVE WORDS

Rather than using generic words that just bounce off your audience, choose emotive words that help them feel what you feel. So instead of saying, "It's great to be here today," say, "I am so thrilled to be here today." (Just make sure you also *look* thrilled—see Chapter 3 on congruence.)

VISIT ONLINE RESOURCES FOR:
A downloadable list of suggestions on emotive words.

TIP 2   ASK FOR AN EMOTIONS CHECK

In person, if people are challenged by what you're saying, often they'll raise their hands and speak up. But in virtual, you have to invite them to do that. Whether you're presenting in person or virtual, stop occasionally and "take the temperature" of your audience. Getting a feel for their emotions works best via open-ended questions, like this: "How does that resonate with you?" or "How does that sit with you?"

These questions prompt reflection and therefore, more meaningful responses.

If you're presenting virtually to a smaller group, encourage people to unmute and share. This can take more time, but better to engage their brains than get through a lot of content quickly.

TIP 3   BE OPEN TO SPONTANEITY

When you're focused on getting through your content, you can miss opportunities to address your audience's needs. Watch out for messages like, "I'm confused" or "I disagree."

> Watch for nonverbal signals that open up opportunities for spontaneous discussion. Try to stay in the moment and respond in real time to what's happening with your group.

TIP 4   PLAY SOME MUSIC

To get your audience talking during group discussions, turn on some tunes. Music relaxes the mind and stimulates creativity, making people feel more confident about sharing. And, research shows playing music during important information helps people more easily recall that information later.

Music paced around 60 beats per minute (the rate of the human heart) is the best choice for small-group discussions and activities that require focus. Apps like Spotify have "bpm playlists" containing songs between 60 and 120 bpm. (You can even experiment with weaving music into your talk around key points you want your audience to remember.) When using music, be sure to keep the sound quality high so it's not just noise.

7.3 The Tools of Connection in Virtual

When it comes to soliciting feedback from your audience, virtual *rules*. Chats, quizzes, polls, breakout rooms, annotation, whiteboards, and even emojis, are all uniquely virtual ways to create an even greater connection with your audience. Let's take a quick look at a range of digital tools commonly used today:

→ **Chat**   Chats quickly build a sense of community by using the back and forth of questions and written feedback. Because they don't involve speaking, they can equalize the conversation between extroverts and introverts. Encourage participants to use chat throughout your presentation to ask questions, share insights, give feedback, and "talk" with one another.

→ **Quiz** Humans love to compete and quizzes are a great way to build engagement by constructively tapping into our innate drive to one-up each other. Use them when you want an energy boost or to enable learning through winning.

→ **Emoji** My nephew (a Gen Zer) can actually text with his buddies using only emojis. This tool concisely captures emotions like jubilation, celebration, or LMAO. Because emojis can clarify tone in the written word, they're a good choice to encourage participants to use along with chat, or when you want to get a quick pulse read on how the audience is feeling.

→ **Poll** If your audience is zoning out, run a poll. Polls can be multiple choice, rating, ranking, word clouds, or just open text. They're a good choice when you want to share insight with your participants or gain usable data for your topic.

→ **Breakout Rooms** Breakout rooms provide participants the opportunity to collaborate by meeting in virtual rooms in small groups. Use these when you want to give your audience a chance to go deeper into your topic. They also allow you to focus on different topics or aspects of a topic at the same time.

→ **Annotation** Annotations are the virtual equivalent of placing an "X" next to your favorite topic on the blackboard. Use these when you want to get a quick group vote or you want to highlight something in a slide.

→ **Digital Whiteboard** These are like standing in front of a conference room whiteboard only better because they provide huge libraries of vibrant images, business planning models, icons, and drawing tools at your fingertips. This is a wonderful tool to use for group brainstorming or building real time visuals as you speak.

These tools can be used together in powerful ways to build connection with an audience.

7.4	**Six Ways to Create a More Inclusive Presentation**

When a speaker is only interested in transmitting, the audience begins to feel like wallpaper: Nice to have, but unnecessary.

> As a speaker, it's important to add small actions that build inclusion, make your audience feel valued and heard, and help them connect to your content (and to you) in a more meaningful, memorable way.

Here are six ways to make people feel welcome:

TIP 1   SAY THEIR NAMES

People love to hear their names. It makes them feel special and recognized. If needed, ask the person for pronunciation help; then jot down your own phonetic spelling, so it's easy to remember. Be sure to call them by their preferred name, and don't assume they like a certain nickname.

TIP 2   TAP INTO EXPERTISE

Ask the group a question and see who demonstrates the greatest knowledge on the topic. Invite those individuals to share their experience.

> Even though you are the expert, recognizing others in the group raises their status and sense of well-being.

TIP 3   SHOW UP EARLY AND BE A GOOD HOST

In virtual presentations, arrive into the meeting at least 15 minutes early and chat with people as they arrive. With live presentations, if you have the opportunity to meet people before your performance, grab it. For example, say yes to a night-before cocktail party or dinner so you can mingle with the guests. Think of this as being the host of the party—your job is to make people feel at ease and welcomed. Be curious. Ask them questions about where they're from and what they want to know about the topic. Introduce people who might benefit from building a connection.

TIP 4   ALLOW OPPORTUNITIES FOR GROUP BRAINSTORMS

Present a challenge and ask the group to brainstorm solutions—even if you know the "right" answer. Rather than giving your verdict on the responses, use a word cloud poll to share answers and ask, "What ideas do you like the most? Why? After seeing this, what other ideas do you have?" Because it taps into group expertise, this is a great way to create a sense of belonging and raise everyone's status. You can use an app like Slido in both live and virtual presentations to run polls and gather ideas.

TIP 5   DEFINE INDUSTRY JARGON OR ACRONYMS

Don't assume everyone will know their meaning. Run your presentation by someone who knows absolutely nothing about the topic and ask them to interrupt you when something doesn't make sense.

TIP 6   AVOID GENDER EXCLUSION

Be mindful of terms like "opposite sex" or "both sexes." Instead, try "people of all genders" or "all genders." If a participant has specified their preferred pronoun, respect them and use it!

Use gender neutral terms. Instead of "you guys," try "people," "folks," "y'all," or "teammates."

7.5 How to Respect Cultural Differences

Take time to learn about the culture of your audience so your message doesn't get lost in accidental etiquette breaches. Are they all from the same location? Do they have a protocol for asking and answering questions? Are certain terms part of their lexicon? A little research can help everyone feel more comfortable.

Before you present, consider the mix of cultures that could describe your audience:

1. **Study the organizational culture.** Start with the website. What are their values and mission? Try to talk with a few people to ask about the culture. Is it formal or informal? Hierarchical or egalitarian? Understanding this will shape your communication.

2. **Embrace the regional culture.** There's a big cultural difference between New York and Los Angeles. New Yorkers tend to be much more direct, whereas Los

Angelenos tend to be less direct and more upbeat. Knowing this, a good speaker will adapt their pace and tone according to which coast is listening.

When you have audiences from around the world, you'll never be able to adjust for every cultural norm, so embrace the differences from the start. Kick off the session with a poll that asks participants to describe their local culture in one word. It's a quick and fun way to build connection, inclusion, and awareness.

3. **Learn the language of your audience (even a little bit).** Does this mean trying to speak a few words of Japanese if you are speaking to a Japanese company? Yes it does. But it also means being present and listening to the words your attendees use when they interact with you. Echo their word choices back to them. If they use the word *standards*, don't change it to *requirements*.

A CLASH OF CULTURES

Taking time to understand how people adapt to culture is *crucial* when two divergent companies from different countries merge. Take, for example, this tale of two companies with two cultures—merging together to initially disastrous results. A US-based tech company acquired another firm rooted in a very different culture, one with a more traditional, formal ethos and a less direct way of communicating. Post-acquisition, the US-based firm formed blended teams from both companies. But they didn't perform the due diligence needed to understand the acquired company's or country's cultures. They didn't introduce the US company's culture to the new employees, or seek employee input on ways to meld together. The expectation? That "new" employees would simply pick up on the acquiring company's culture, and assimilate to blend in. Within a year, both companies were hemorrhaging talent, running crisis control on costly communication mistakes, and struggling with absenteeism and low morale. I was brought in to form a new approach. We got down to fundamentals: explicitly understanding, respecting, and celebrating the unique and separate cultures. And executing a strategy to tap *all* employees for ways to blend the best of both organizations. Within 18 months, attrition dropped by 30 percent, and morale plus engagement rose by 40 percent.

EXERCISE:
PRACTICE MIRRORING

Multiple studies show that when primates are in harmony, they tend to mirror each other's body language, speaking tones and patterns, and (in humans) word choices. It's the brain's way of saying, "I am one of you. I belong with you."

I lived in London for several years. Brits always spotted me as a Yank the minute I opened my mouth. But at home in the United States, people would ask, "Where are you from? You don't have an American accent." I do have an American accent, but the way I spoke when living in the UK had shifted to mirror the people around me.

There's a difference between mirroring and mimicking, though. You don't want your sincere attempt at connection to backfire into a caricature of easy stereotypes.

Connecting with your audience means they will be more alert, feel more positive, and be more likely to remember your message. But giving your audience a voice isn't all hand-holding and campfire songs. When you open the floor to questions, you have to be ready to answer them—and some can be tough. In Chapter 9, we'll talk about how questions (even the uncomfortable ones) can be used to your advantage.

CHAPTER SUMMARY
KEY TAKEAWAYS:

- Your audience wants to be engaged with, not talked at.

- Set the expectation that your talk will be interactive, so attendees can become participants who are mentally prepared to speak up.

- Be intentional about planning connection into your presentation by using engagement tools such as polls, whiteboards, chats, and quizzes.

CHAPTER 8

Words

At our core, we speak because we want or need something.

So, if we want our needs met via our presentations, word choice is critical. It's not just what we say, but *how* we say it. Use too many words, and we bore or confuse our listeners. Employ language that's too complex, and we risk making our audience feel lectured or demeaned. Aim to be too simple, and we sound patronizing. Whether ordering a coffee or rallying a team, the words we use matter.

Let's examine word choice through the lenses of **brevity and clarity**—two areas where I see most presenters struggle. To be succinct and clear, each of your ideas must crisply and lucidly build on one another.

8.1 Use Brevity and Clarity to Improve Overall Message Impact

Why do we talk too much? Sometimes it is due to nerves or anxiety. *Most* of the time, it's because we're not being clear, so we feel like we must keep explaining. We think more words help clarify our ideas. But in reality, more words can reduce the listeners' confidence in your expertise. And if you're not clear on what you're saying, your audience will not be clear either.

Each of the following tips will simplify and clarify your word choice, so audiences are more deeply engaged in your core ideas:

TIP 1   SPEAK TO THE GAP

Always consider your audience first, focusing on the gap between what they know and what you *need* them to know. What's in the gap of knowing and not knowing? For example, senior executives might not need a bunch of background on a topic, so the presentation can focus on the problem and suggested solution. *Mind the gap.*

TIP 2   BEGIN WITH THE END IN MIND

In a sentence, what is the *one* idea you want the audience to walk out of the room with? Now phrase it as one sentence of seven words or less, like a newspaper headline. Cut nonessential words, and get to the heart of your take-home message. This core message then becomes the foundation of your presentation.

STORY:
BELIEVABILITY THROUGH BREVITY

Television interviews demand punchy comments and tweetable quotes. But a senior executive at a global tech firm was told he turned off audiences by talking too much. Our coaching uncovered the culprit: not nerves, but passion. He loved his work . . . and it made him chatty! He'd talk, and then talk some more, hoping to spread his passion. Instead, he turned people off. We focused on his seeing brevity as a critical channel to trust building. So, once this expert began answering hosts' questions with his pithiest, most tweetable headlines, he garnered more engagement.

TIP 3   GRAB THEM WITH THE INTRO

Without a strong start, your audience will quickly check out. For example:

"Good morning. It's great to be here today, and thank you for having me. Today I'm going to talk to you about how you can increase your sales. First, we'll look at what's challenging about selling in the virtual world; next we'll look at what your prospective clients want in a virtual sales meeting. Finally, we'll look at five tools to give clients what they want. And then I'll take questions."

This intro uses the classic "tell them what you're going to tell them, tell them, and then tell them what you told them" structure. Unfortunately, it also puts people to sleep because it's formulaic and uninteresting. Instead, a good introduction grabs the audience's attention and builds interest. How can you accomplish that? By using four methods . . .

8.2	**Four Ways to Create a More Engaging Opening**

METHOD 1   CHALLENGE THEM TO THINK

Ask a question. Engage your audience by asking a question relevant to your topic. It might be around their personal experience about the subject. Using a question at the top immediately tells them they're in for an interactive experience. You can also ask a rhetorical question to move them from listener to participant. For example, "What would happen if you joined us in this change initiative?"

METHOD 2   USE A GUIDING METAPHOR

Metaphors help speed understanding by leveraging a universal reference that links the known to the unknown. If you want people to *see* what you're saying, climb aboard the metaphor train. Metaphors help us internalize ideas in pictures so we can remember them more effectively.

FEATURE:
YOU CAN LITERALLY GRASP A HAND. YOU CAN ALSO METAPHORICALLY GRASP A CONCEPT

"People use a metaphor every 20 words," suggests Dr. Vicky Lai, University of Arizona assistant professor of psychology and cognitive science.[6] Studies show that when we use metaphors like "She had a rough day," regions of the brain associated with tactile experience are activated. If you say, "He's a salty old sailor," areas associated with taste are activated. And when we use verbs, such as "grasp a concept," motor perception and planning activate.

METHOD 3   ENGAGE THEIR EMOTIONS

Tell a brief story. Stories can be case studies, personal experiences, or analogies. Just make sure your story is clearly linked to your content and has a strong emotional hook. For example: "I'm a research oncologist. I develop life-saving drugs and work to understand a patient's journey in fighting this disease. But last year, my sister was diagnosed with cancer, and suddenly this became very personal."

Split a story. You can introduce the story at the top of your talk, then leave the audience on the edge of their seat with a cliffhanger. Don't finish the story until the end of the talk.

Share a quote. By referencing a well-known person or expert, you establish a connection with your listeners: "I know them!"

METHOD 4   MAKE A PROVOCATIVE STATEMENT

A strong beginning grabs your audience's attention at the top and says, "Here's why you should listen to me for the next hour." And once you hook them, make sure you *keep* them hooked by choosing the shortest, sharpest words.

State a problem. When you start with what's wrong, the audience is engaged because they're listening for your solution. You can combine this with a story or statistic that grabs their attention. "Covid-19 has pushed women's workforce participation to a 30-year low. Welcome back to the 1980s, everyone."

Lay down the gauntlet. A simple, declarative statement can shock listeners to attention. I call this "laying down the gauntlet." Make a direct but bold statement that challenges the audience to think or feel differently about the topic. Then, set out to support your gauntlet statement. During his speech for the rededication of the Eternal Light Peace Memorial at Gettysburg National Cemetery in 1998, Carl Sagan opened his speech with: "Fifty-one thousand human beings were killed or wounded here, ancestors of some of us, brothers of us all."[7]

8.3   How to Craft the Body of Your Presentation

As you write the body of your talk, you may be tempted to fill a presentation with every exhaustive detail because you *love* this stuff. Don't. Keep to *three* points.

> A great presentation focuses on the "must-haves" instead of the "should or could haves."

Here, support your main point with data, analogies, stories, and examples. As you think about your three points, consider:

1. **Must, aka the three-minute version.** What's *most* critical for your audience to know about this topic? If you only had three minutes, what information would you share with them?

2. **Should, aka the seven-minute version.** What *should* they know about the topic? This content is still relatively critical. If your talk was cut from 30 minutes to 10, this is information you'd keep.

3. **Could, aka the sharing-a-bottle-of-wine version.** If you had all day (and night), what *could* they learn about the topic? This falls under the category of, "Oh that's cool/

interesting/wow." If you have loads of time, this approach can be handy. Though you might be better off using extra time to ask for questions from the audience.

Aim for long, medium, and short versions of your talk, just in case you need to cut or add things, depending on time. If you have more time, you can dive into the body of your talk with more detail. Maybe one point has three subpoints. But if you're short on time, your 10-minute version just covers highlights of each.

8.4 Crafting a Memorable Conclusion

Don't kick off the conclusion by saying "in conclusion" or "in summary." Add some drama and engagement by taking a nice big pause, and returning to the beginning. Then, leave them with how you want them to feel or act. Rephrase your take-home message and bring it to a close by leaving one final thought and feeling.

At the end of your presentation, your audience will be trying to remember what they've just heard, so help them. A brief summary of your key points tells them exactly what they should take away from your talk.

The best way to summarize is to engage *their* brains while you do it. Ask for key insights they've gleaned from what you've said, and discuss what they felt was most relevant. You can do this with a poll, via thoughts in the chat, or even by going into breakout rooms. If you feel they missed a critical idea, add it.

A great close doesn't mean you need to repeat everything you've just said. Just ask yourself, "What do I want the audience to think, feel, do, or believe after this talk?" Give them a strong call to action, thank them, and enjoy the moment of a job well done.

TIP:
WHAT I REALLY WANT TO SAY IS . . .

It's challenging to stick only to the most critical information, especially when we feel passionate about a topic. If you're struggling to find those key ideas, my friend and colleague Rena Cook has a great tool. Ask yourself, "What I really want to say is . . ." and then in one sentence, just spit it out—in writing or into a recorder.

Use this tool when planning your talk or when struggling to find your main idea or key points. You can fine-tune later. I wrote my entire thesis this way. It works.

8.5 (Tremendous) Tips for Choosing Better Words

Our language is filled with modifiers that don't add anything. Instead of saying, "It's really, really good," say "It's phenomenal." Instead of saying, "It's very bad," describe *why*. Is it dangerous? A waste of resources? Boring?

TIP 1 USE NAAV WORDS

A good place to start with making your language come alive is NAAV words (nouns, adjectives, adverbs, and verbs). These are the words or phrases that 1) move the action forward, 2) infuse emotion and sensory experience, and 3) are most relevant to our audience.

 VISIT ONLINE RESOURCES FOR:
Tips on using NAAV words.

TIP 2 HEADLINE YOUR TALK

Think of a newspaper headline for each section of content. If you were to jump from headline to headline, what would that sound like? Next, consider which of your headlines are most important. Can you eliminate or reduce content from sections under the other headlines? When you boil down sections to their key ideas, it's easier to compare their value and prioritize what to keep.

TIP 3 CHOOSE VIBRANT LANGUAGE

Brevity isn't just about using fewer words; it's about finding the *right* words to convey our meaning. Unfortunately, when many of us present, we focus too much on pragmatic, safer, and more familiar language. But if we allow our talk to take on an epic scale—with urgency and drama—our word choice is transformed, and the story becomes vivid, graphic, and compelling.

TIP 4 LET GO OF USELESS WORDS

When we practice using words that are alive—words that carry meaning, action, sound, feeling, taste, seeing, and emotion—we learn to eliminate frivolous modifiers. Consider the difference between these words:

Nice	Pleasant
Interesting	Engrossing
A lot	Enormous
Really-really	Intensely
Good	Delightful
Fine	Gratifying

TIP 5 USE MORE EMOTIVE LANGUAGE

Because the virtual world flattens voices and reduces visual cues, we can help our audience by infusing our language with emotional words. Consider the difference between, "It's great to be here today," and "I'm thrilled/delighted/honored to be here today."

⬇ **VISIT ONLINE RESOURCES FOR:**
A list of emotive words.

EXERCISE: WRITE POETRY

Poetry works because it distills an idea, action, image, or emotion into one or a few words. Reading and writing poetry teaches us to choose words that count because they stimulate the senses.

Try this: Write a phrase like "he was really, really busy" and then start to list out new phrases that capture how busy he was:

→ He was busy as a grasshopper in late summer.

→ He was maniacally busy.

→ He was hustling busy.

→ He was on the go.

→ He worked nonstop.

→ He was drowning in paperwork.

Now think through your presentation. What key messages could be more engaging and more memorable with an upgrade to more vibrant language?

TIP 6   AVOID CLICHÉS AND JARGON LIKE THE PLAGUE

"Fruit" and "ocean" are indeed lovely words. But "low-hanging fruit" and "boiling the ocean" are overused business clichés.

Worn-out expressions erode your credibility as an innovative communicator.

Jargon creates an exclusionary environment because those who understand it will feel part of the in-crowd. Everyone else will most likely not understand you, yet think they *should*, and then remain quiet as they try to figure out what the heck you're saying.

When you have no way to express an idea except to use technical language, make sure to define your terms, but keep definitions to a minimum. Remember to keep your language plainspoken, so everyone in the crowd can understand. Instead of saying, "This is where the rubber meets the road," say, "The most important step begins here." Compelling language is immediate, direct, and clear.

STORY:
JARRING JARGON

I sat in the audience, watching a presentation by a senior tech executive at one of the largest technology consulting firms in the world. My client was considering working with the organization and had asked me to watch their presentation. The talk was going well, but then the speaker said, "We need to keep an eye out for folks who go off the reservation." My stomach lurched. I could hear audible gasps around me. I was sure the speaker could hear them as well. But then he used the offensive remark again.

And then a third time. He clearly had no idea of this phrase's deeply painful history. My client and I sat in disbelief and anger—how could he be so unaware?

Moral of the story: Don't let yourself get into this situation. Best rule of thumb: if you're uncertain on jargon, leave it out.

8.6   The Art of Storytelling

Stories are the oldest form of communication and persuasion. Humans tell stories to teach, share history, and persuade others. Stories are compelling because the listener can put themselves in the shoes of the main character. Using stories in your presentation helps listeners digest your content in memorable, shareable bits.

Remember the monkey from Chapter 3 whose brain lit up when the researcher ate a peanut? That's what stories do to our brains. Our mirror neurons light up when we hear a good story. We feel the same emotions, and sometimes even *experience* the same physical sensations, as the main characters.

Think of the last time you watched a scary movie. Chances are, the moment the villain came too close to the heroine, your heart rate and breathing increased. That's your brain's mirror neurons relating to the heroine.

Humans love to find out what happens at each turn of a story, so the tales we tell keep our audience's brains maximally engaged. To practice this, start with a simple story, like something embarrassing that happened to you. What happened first, next, last? Then, try an epic story. It might be one of survival or a personal odyssey, where there is a cost or a conflict. You can even turn a client case story into an epic tale of survival, challenge, and growth—a hero's journey.

VISIT ONLINE RESOURCES FOR:
An exercise on how to tell a good story.

Your words don't just define the nuts and bolts of your content; they determine how your audience will *experience* your message. When choosing the expressions for sharing your ideas, remember that it's not just what you say, but *how you say it.*

**CHAPTER SUMMARY
KEY TAKEAWAYS:**

- Structure your talk to create the most engaging story and avoid overexplaining.

- Improve the impact of your delivery by choosing more powerful, more emotive words.

- Add stories and stats to open and close your talk with urgency, drama, and clarity.

PART THREE

Engagement

CHAPTER 9

Questions

There you are. Humming right along with your presentation when someone has the audacity to raise their hand. Just when you were building toward the really good part, too. How dare they be confused/challenging/excited/curious right now? Your content is crystal clear. Your delivery is well-paced. Yet, there it is. The hand.

Questions can feel like an unwanted interruption. They can also be a wonderful tool of communication. They're how we see things from other people's perspectives, and how we make sure our content is being understood, not just heard. But questions can also be flustering if you're not prepared to field them.

When you're in control of the questions, you can use them to start conversations, gauge comprehension, and guide deeper dives into content. When your audience is in control of the questions, however, your role can quickly change from sharer of wisdom to defender of the chart on slide six.

With a few strategies for thinking on your feet, not only can you learn how to address questions, but also how to love them for what they are—validation that your audience is engaged.

9.1 How to Get Better at Anticipating Questions

You know there will be questions, so what will they be? Think through your presentation from the audience's perspective and try to anticipate what they might ask. Don't go easy on yourself, either.

> Surfacing tough, even combative, questions will help you prepare for surprises— intellectually and emotionally.

Maybe they'll never get asked, but if they do, you can respond with a level head and a solid answer.

Ask yourself:

1. What's the one question I hope they don't ask, and how will I address it?

2. If I were in their shoes, what would I want to know?

3. If I disagreed with something, what would it be?

> If you can identify several questions for a certain section, consider addressing them preemptively within your content.

You can say, "One question you might have here is . . ." or "The first time I heard about this, I wondered about . . ." You can also request questions from the audience in advance. When people register, ask, "What's your burning question on this topic?" This helps you tailor content to their needs and gets you ready for Q&A.

9.2   Defining a Structure for Answers

When a question pops up while you're presenting, you not only have to think of the answer, but how to deliver it, too. Using a structure for your answers will keep your answers succinct and on point. Here's a simple structure to consider:

→ **Focus**: Focus on one main point only, so it's easier for your audience to comprehend.

→ **Proof**: Back up your point with proof (i.e., research and statistics). If you don't have data, explain why you believe it to be true and speak from the heart.

→ **Support**: Highlight a brief example that supports your main point.

→ **Notice**: Check for understanding. Do they still look confused? If so, paraphrase your main point another way.

KNOW WHAT YOU'RE ANSWERING

It can be helpful to paraphrase the main point of the question before answering it, so you're clear about what is being asked. Say, "I think you're asking about X. Is that right?" Then allow time for the questioner to respond. They may not choose to speak up, but invite them all the same.

THEY'RE NERVOUS, TOO

A recent Slido survey found that 54 percent of respondents said they prefer to ask questions anonymously in virtual events. Letting people ask questions privately gives everyone equal opportunity to participate. A simple way to offer anonymity is to invite questions by private chat message. Some platforms, such as Zoom, allow you to set up permissions in advance for participants to ask questions anonymously.

> Your audience may be as nervous about asking questions as you are about answering them.

FROM CONFRONTATIONAL TO CONNECTED

Dinesh was a brilliant anesthesiologist and research scientist who treated nearly every question as a personal challenge to his expertise, putting him at odds with the audience. "They just want to discredit me and make themselves feel smarter," he assumed, as he barked responses. In the one presentation I viewed on video, he looked angry, defensive, even a little scary . . . which only made his audience more antagonistic. Because scrutinizing research is fundamental to being a great scientist, we needed a more helpful frame for how Dinesh viewed questions. So, as his coach, I asked: "What if you viewed every question as critical, natural, and even a fun *opportunity* to engage? What if each time, you said to yourself, "Yeah . . . c'mon. Bring it ON! This is going to be fun!" He began experimenting with this, in a low-risk environment. The difference? Night and day! He made eye contact, stood up straighter, and even *smiled* at people. He looked like he *wanted* to be there. Best of all, he remained in command, rather than become railroaded. So, next time you feel intimidated or pissed off at a question, ask how you can reframe the confrontation as an opportunity to connect and learn.

9.3	How to End with a Solid Q&A Session

Running a Q&A session at the end of a presentation can be one of the most important interactive moments you can create with your audience. It's another way for participants to be actively involved in the content and dive deeper into the topics they care about.

To make a kick-ass Q&A, collect questions throughout the presentation.

People can easily forget what they wanted to ask if they don't share it in the moment. At the start of your session, if your session is virtual, announce that the chat will be open throughout your time together so questions can be captured as they arise.

As questions come in, you can address them in real time or save them until the end. But even if you don't answer in real time, try to at least acknowledge that they've been submitted. Say something like, "Thanks, Chris, that's an important question, and I'll address it by the end." Or, "My producer is telling me we've got questions coming in. We'll pause and get to those in about five minutes."

If you have a large audience from whom you expect heaps of questions, ask your producer to respond to them with a private chat text, such as, "Thank you, John. We will address your question in just a few minutes." With a larger audience, you won't have the mental space to focus on every question as it is submitted.

If a question is around technical issues or confusion around instructions, address them right away! The person won't be able to focus on what you're saying if they are sidetracked with difficulties.

HOW TO MAKE ANY Q&A SESSION MORE PRODUCTIVE

What if no one asks a question? This is one of the most common worries that I hear from speakers thinking through their Q&A sessions. Here are a few tips for both managing this fear, and setting up any Q&A session for success:

TIP 1   KICK OFF THE Q&A BY ASKING A POINTED QUESTION YOURSELF

For example, rather than ask, "Are there any questions?" try, "Who has a question about the first insight?" Or, "What are your thoughts on that?" Or "Who's had this experience before?" Or, "One question I'm often asked is . . . "

TIP 2   CREATE A DEDICATED TIME FOR PARTICIPANTS TO COME UP WITH QUESTIONS

When you reach the end of a section, invite reflection and questions. "Take 30 seconds now to think about what you've just heard and share a question with the person sitting to your left (or in virtual presentations: write your questions in the chat function. Or raise your hand to come off mute and speak to the group)."

TIP 3   LET YOUR AUDIENCE PRIORITIZE THE QUESTIONS

Once all questions are submitted, display them anonymously in a poll and have the audience vote on their top three to five favorites for you to address. Or use a tool like Slido to automatically crowdsource the audience's most burning queries.

| 9.4 | **Managing the Scary Side of Q&A** |

When we open the session to Q&A, we give up some control to the questioners—and that can be downright scary. Participants can ask highly detailed questions, give comments framed as questions, or outright challenge your authority. This can make you feel anxious, defensive, or angry.

> Since losing your cool can erode credibility, you need to stay on track by handling tough questions gracefully.

1. **Breathe and manage your own emotions.** When we become upset, emotions can keep us from making rational decisions. Simply breathing and saying to yourself, "Okay, I'm feeling a little defensive here," can help keep your brain out of emotional highjack. This is called affect labeling. When we name how we're feeling, it activates the brain's control centers and actually dampens the emotion.

VISIT ONLINE RESOURCES FOR:
A downloadable guide to read more about emotion or affect labeling.

2. **Keep your message in sight.** Always have a sticky note in your field of vision that has your take-home message on it. Remind yourself of the message and ask, "Does this question support my take-home message?" If not, manage your response to move away from the question and back on track.

3. **Reframe how you view their behavior.** Audiences' nerves might make them ramble, they might like to hear themselves talk, or perhaps they just want to share something with the group. It doesn't help you to frame their behavior negatively. It does help you to remain composed, kind, respectful, and in control of the session.

> Remind yourself that most of the time, audience members aren't actually trying to derail your presentation.

9.5 Prepare Some Memorized Responses

Having a few memorized responses to fall back on will help you manage tricky moments.

MEMORIZED RESPONSE	USEFUL FOR
"Thank you for that insight; lots of good things to consider there."	The expert who gives a long-winded comment in the guise of a question.
"Thank you for your feedback. I'd love to talk with you more about this afterward."	When someone gives you negative feedback or is trying to derail your presentation or undermine your credibility. Do not get in an argument with the person. Do not debate. Simply thank them for the feedback and move on.
"Thank you for your question. That requires a detailed answer, so let's connect afterward and I will help you with that."	When someone asks a detailed question and it will take too long to answer. Or if answering only has value for the questioner, but not the rest of the audience.

MEMORIZED RESPONSE	USEFUL FOR
"I'm going to pause you there. What's your question?"	When you've got a questioner who's recreating their own oral history behind the question they want to ask. Wait for a pause in their speaking and then respectfully ask them this.
"Thank you for that comment. Let's move to the next person."	When someone starts to ramble on with an irrelevant comment with no question. Again, wait for the person to take a breath or pause, then gently say this.
"I'm so glad you brought that up because we are going to talk about just that today."	Also called bridging, this is useful when you have a rambler on your hands. Wait for the pause, and then use something they've just mentioned to bridge to your next topic.

Questions are an important part of any communication. In virtual presentations they are especially helpful in keeping you and your audience on the same page.

By giving questions your attention before, during, and after your session, you show your audience you appreciate their participation and value their curiosity.

CHAPTER SUMMARY
KEY TAKEAWAYS:

- Prepare for questions before they're asked and have a few memorized phrases to handle the trickier ones.

- Follow a repeatable structure for your answers.

- Create a productive Q&A session by managing questions from the beginning.

CHAPTER 10

Visuals

Visuals help our audience process and retain content. Sadly, nowadays, this often means a deck—that is, a grouping—of PowerPoint slides. You know the formula: bullet points, an icon/picture, slide title, logo—and a bored or confused audience.

It doesn't have to be that way. Instead of overwhelming your audience with a reading assignment on every slide, think visually.

Great visuals include everything from sketches on napkins to photos of world issues to funny video clips.

> Visuals connect with people emotionally, in a way bullet points can't, and they instantly create feelings of joy, pride, and even anger.

As a participant in one of my workshops described it, "The job of visuals is to simplify, amplify, and clarify!"

Microsoft estimates that 95 percent of business presentations are created using PowerPoint, with 500 million people around the world using it to give 30 million presentations every day.[8] Wow! That's a lotta slides. We all use slides. We just need to use them better.

10.1 How to Simplify Your Visuals

Here are four tips for improving and simplifying your slides:

TIP 1 ONE IDEA, ONE SLIDE

The human brain can only focus on and comprehend one idea at a time, and it quickly loses interest when barraged with bullet points.[9] So keep your slides to one idea per slide. This means one graph, one statistic, one chart, one visual at a time.

> If you have more than one idea, create a new slide.

Change

- CHANGE is a natural part of the work world — there is no avoiding it.
- Everyone responds to change differently — from "change junkie" to being very fearful or uncomfortable with change.
- If we can better understand what we go through during times of change, we can better manage it by DEVELOPING COPING STRATEGIES.

Change is the only constant in life.

- Heraclitus

TIP 2   STOP THE HOSTAGE TAKING

Our brains can't read and listen at the same time, and they read faster than we speak. If you're reading your bullets out loud, your audience will feel trapped while they wait for you to catch up. Avoid this by cutting text altogether and using a visual that speaks to your main point. If you absolutely must have words, keep it to a simple headline.

TIP 3   USE POINTERS, BUT JUDICIOUSLY

If you're showing a complicated visual, like a graph or chart, you can use the pointer or pen tool to highlight what you want your audience to focus on but keep it simple. Click on the area, then click off or, when presenting virtually, use the annotation tool.

TIP 4   MOVE IT ALONG

Don't stay on one slide for too long.

Frequent screen changes with new material pull the audience's attention back from other distractions.

Slides should support what you're saying, but they're not a script. Visual slides can make your talk more emotional, clearer, and memorable. You're not there to read. You're there to engage.

10.2	**How to Move from Slides to Visuals**

Visuals amplify emotions and key ideas. And they don't always need to be PowerPoint slides. When using visuals, think about what you want your audience to feel. A study at the Wharton Research Center showed that participants remember 50 percent of visual information but only 5 percent of bulleted information.[10]

If you want people to remember what you're saying, amplify it with something memorable to look at, such as an unexpected prop.

STORY:
FLIPPING ON STAGE

A few years ago, I was coaching TEDx speaker and Parkour designer Colin MacDonald for his talk on the power of physical play for adults. Parkour is about movement—creating spaces, particularly in overlooked parts of cities, where adults are encouraged to jump, skip, slide, run, dance, and play.

In our rehearsals, I noticed Colin had the impulse to move as he was speaking, but he felt constrained by that "red carpet dot" of the TED stage. We started to brainstorm how he could bring movement into his talk, and ultimately landed on bringing a small Parkour design on stage with him. The talk came alive. Rather than talking about movement, he moved while he talked, and the audience could experience it with him. (See his talk, "Designing a more playful city," at tedxseattle.com.)

That's the power of props—using a physical object to bring an idea alive.

EXAMPLES OF TALKS WITH PROPS

SPEAKER	TALK	PROP USED
Bill Gates	Mosquitos, malaria, and education	Mosquitos
Ava Holmes	Blue jeans or blue water: Fashion powering conservation around the world	Fashion models
Dananjaya Hettiarachchi	2014 Toastmasters World Champion of Public Speaking	Flower
Aji Piper	Kids sue the government to fight climate change—and win	Ukulele
Judy Twedt	Connecting to climate change through music	Piano
Richard Sears	Planning for the end of oil	Oil, limestone, chalk, and more

> Props make points more emotional and memorable. They can be physical objects, or they can be metaphors.

Props help make abstract ideas concrete. They add the element of surprise because most people show up to a presentation expecting slides!

> Are you talking about a *thing*? Bring it *into* your presentation, and *use* it rather than just talking about it.

But avoid babies and cute animals; they'll steal the show every time.

You can even send your audience the item before your virtual presentation and have them use it *with* you.

When you use a prop:

→ Plan for when you will use it, and have it easily within reach.

→ Pick it up, use it, and then put it down, preferably out of sight.

→ When you pick it up, be careful not to hit the mic and overwhelm the audience's ears.

→ Don't have it in hand if you're not actually using it.

→ Avoid fiddling with it.

→ Use it with purpose so it supports your message instead of distracting from it.

10.3 Should You Use Video in Your Presentation?

Videos are persuasive because they combine music, story, imagery, and character to grab attention and build emotion. They can make us laugh, cry, and feel angry, inspired, or hopeful. All of these emotions spark action.

STORY:
VIDEO VIGNETTES

An example of the power of videography, from a workshop I led on women's leadership: I showed a video about nine-year-old Riley Morrison writing to basketball star Steph Curry about why his shoes weren't available in girls' sizes. It was a succinct, convincing way to illustrate how leadership can come from anyone, at any time. Such a vignette resonated deeply, especially because the audience included a lot of moms and dads.

> To find great video content, you don't have to rely solely on movies. Sources like YouTube, Vimeo, Instagram, IGTV, Twitch, and TikTok (to name a few) also offer lots of great videos.

WARNING: When using any copyrighted material, be aware of how and when you can legally use it.

VISIT ONLINE RESOURCES FOR:
Suggested articles on how to use copyrighted material.

WHAT TO REMEMBER WHEN USING VIDEO IN A PRESENTATION

→ Know the point you're trying to illustrate. Teamwork? Innovation? Resilience? Leadership? Then find the video or clip that fits.

→ Keep it short—no longer than three minutes.

→ Show it at the right time:

- At the beginning to grab attention and set the mood

- At the end to spark a specific action from the audience

- In the middle to illustrate a point or generate discussion and debate

If online uploading speed is a nonissue, it's hard to beat the emotional punch video provides. Or avoid low-bandwidth issues by downloading the video file into your deck.

10.4 How to Clarify Ideas with Visuals

Visuals clarify our thinking because they take those wonderfully, sometimes abstract, ideas floating around in our heads and give us something concrete to look at and work with. That's why we use things like whiteboards or handouts—so we can *see* what we're thinking and talking about.

VIRTUAL WHITEBOARDS

Whiteboards keep the audience in the moment by giving you and them a blank slate to create content as it happens. This gives your presentation a spontaneous, fresh feel.

Most virtual whiteboards have many built-in creativity tools: images, icons, reactions, voting, drawing, Post-it Notes, embedded videos. You can even create a digital version of a flipchart. Plus, asking your audience to collaborate and write their own content can help them remember your talk, since research shows writing by hand helps people process information better.[11]

You can also use a good, old-fashioned whiteboard behind you. If you do, make sure your webcam has a high enough resolution that your audience can see it. And, be sure to write *large* and legibly.

HANDOUTS

If you feel like you need to cram a bunch of information on a slide, first ask yourself: What information does my audience really *need*? (See Chapter 8 for tips on brevity.) If you decide the additional information is crucial, create a handout.

Ways to use handouts:

➜ As a cheat-sheet of tips and key takeaways from your talk.

➜ As instructional support during breakouts.

➜ As a presentation preview. Ask the audience to read a handout before the event and jot down ideas, questions, and preferences for their desired areas of focus. Or give them a few minutes to scan the document as the meeting begins.

Whether you use PowerPoint or poster board, make sure it's interesting. Think of each blank page as an opportunity to help your audience experience your message in a more memorable way.

CHAPTER SUMMARY
KEY TAKEAWAYS:

- Don't use slides just to repeat your verbal content.

- Ask yourself: How can the right visual simplify, amplify, and clarify my message?

- Take a break from slides and incorporate other interesting things to look at, like props, whiteboards, videos, and handouts.

PART FOUR

Details

Alice just loves moderating panels,
especially when there is a healthy disagreement.

CHAPTER 11

Presenting with Others

Whether you're co-presenting, participating in a panel discussion, or serving as an emcee, many of the techniques discussed in earlier chapters are applicable. Transitioning from solo artist to ensemble comes with some challenges, though. The following strategies will help you navigate these situations with the same confidence as in your one-person show.

11.1 Co-Presenting

Tandem presentations take practice, but can be a lot of fun when you're with someone you enjoy. A few benefits of presenting together:

→ Relieves some of the pressure of having the whole show on your shoulders

→ Makes it easier to monitor the audience while the other person is speaking

→ Brings your audience two speakers' perspectives on the same topic

→ Different voices and speaking styles help keep the audience's attention

Whenever you're co-presenting, two steps are critical:

First, define clear roles. Who is taking what content? When? Who handles which types of questions?

Second, rehearse. Do at least one dry run before the actual presentation, and:

→ Consider what could go wrong and how you'll manage it.

→ Check sound, cameras, lighting—any tools you'll be using.

→ If you're using breakout rooms, practice going into, leaving, and switching between them.

→ Do a practice Q&A, and assign types of questions to each speaker.

→ Practice handoffs between speakers.

When presenting virtually, these four tips will help ensure a smooth ride:

TIP 1 WORK FROM A MASTER SCRIPT

Multiple PowerPoint decks increase the risk of someone's slides not working. So, you'll be more effective with just one set of slides. Many video conference platforms now offer a remote-control feature, which ensures a seamless handover of control for advancing the slides. Be sure to practice the hand-off and transition so they're smooth.

TIP 2 SYNC YOUR AUDIO AND VIDEO

Ensure all speakers have similar volumes, camera angles, and lighting. You don't want to be louder or softer, or harder or easier to see, than your partner. Otherwise, your audience will be distracted as they try to adjust for the difference.

TIP 3 SET UP A COMMUNICATION CHANNEL

Whether it's WhatsApp, Facebook Messenger, Slack, or texting, agree on a back-channel form for all speakers and moderators, via which you will communicate during the event. Then you can stay in touch with each other as needed. Be sure to check that everyone has notifications turned on before you go live. And silence any other device alarms, so they don't interrupt your presentation.

TIP 4 ENSURE ALL SPEAKERS PARTICIPATE IN Q&A, ESPECIALLY IF IT'S AT THE END

If only two are people speaking, it's fun to treat the Q&A as a conversation: one speaker reads a question, the other one answers it, and then switch.

11.2 Seven Techniques for Better Panel Discussions

Panels are best when there's robust discussion among the panelists, adeptly orchestrated by a master moderator. We've all attended the snooze-fest panel discussions where each speaker is given a few minutes to talk, the moderator adds zero perspective, and it feels like a series of boring, disconnected mini-speeches. If you're doing a virtual panel, there's the added challenge of missing the buzz of in-person energy. The result can feel like a visit to Madame Tussauds' Wax Museum.

Whether live or virtual, when you're a panelist, be the courteous guest, the interesting, fun, self-aware one. Be the guest about whom everyone says, "Oh yes, she was a pleasure to have here."

Here's how to add to a more robust conversation and stand out when you're part of a panel:

TIP 1 SPEAK IN SOUND BITES

You can help the moderator encourage audience engagement by clarifying your key ideas into Tweetable, bite-sized phrases. What do you want your audience to remember about your topic? Write it down. Now write a few Tweets on the topic. (Hint: if you're doing a virtual presentation, you can keep these in your field of vision throughout the discussion to help you remember them.)

TIP 2   STAY IN YOUR LANE

Has the moderator asked a question that doesn't come close to your point of view? Then pass on it. Let another panelist speak to it. Stick to responding to questions that give you the opportunity to speak with conviction and consequence.

TIP 3   LOOK FOR DISAGREEMENT

Disagreement is attention-grabbing, but agree to disagree agreeably.

> Use "yes and . . ." to disagree and build on what your colleague has said.

Instead of, "Yes, but Alice has this all wrong," try: "I like what Alice said about digital transformation and rapid change being the new normal, *and* I also think it's important we allow time for employees to celebrate and acknowledge when they've successfully delivered on change."

TIP 4   BE THE MASTER OF YOUR UNIVERSE

In person, the technology is covered by the production team. In virtual, it's *your* job. So, test your technology before you log in to the meeting. Make sure your internet, mic, camera, and lighting are set up and working.

TIP 5   GIVE THE GIFT OF BREVITY

Ask the moderator how much time they would like spent on comments, and don't rely on the host to tell you when your time is up. Keep an eye on the clock, and wrap up any comment before they have to cut you off. Let the moderator or the audience ask a follow-up question if they want to learn more.

TIP 6   STAY ALERT

It's important to maintain your attention and focus. When you can, jot notes on what fellow panelists say so you can refer back to them. Be ready to listen actively.

TIP 7   SPEAK TO ALL AUDIENCES

In an in-person panel discussion, eye contact alternates back and forth among fellow panelists, the moderator, and the audience. If you're virtual, be deliberate and specific about whom you're addressing. Whether virtual or live, ensure you're including all audiences by:

→ Using names to direct your comments.

→ Learning about the audience beforehand and speaking to specific audience segments in your comments.

→ Looking for ways to weave the comments of your fellow panelists (along with their names) into your remarks.

→ Always speaking into the camera, if your event is virtual. If you're speaking at a hybrid event, make a point of occasionally looking right into the camera that's simulcasting your talk, so the virtual attendees feel seen.

11.3	How to Master the Chaos as a Moderator

It may seem as if moderators must be natural ambassadors, generous listeners, gifted conversationalists, *and* deliver endless patience. But actually, you just have to be prepared.

> Invited to be a moderator? You needn't be superhuman. You just need a plan.

Here are a few ideas to help:

TIP 1 STICK TO YOUR EXPERTISE

Accept the invitation to moderate a panel on topics on which you have experience or expertise, so you can add value and ask insightful questions.

TIP 2 MIX IT UP

Tap into tools from Chapters 9, 10, and 11 to maintain attention and engagement. Poll or quiz the audience, conduct a lightning round of quick answers from the panelists, or take questions from the audience. Use sentence starters to get everyone engaged, such as, "I knew I was in trouble in my presentation when . . ." Mix up how you engage everyone by alternating the activities you do together.

TIP 3   SHARE A SHOW-FLOW

By sharing a show-flow with your panelists, they'll have a rough estimate of timing and corresponding events. It might look something like this:

→ 11:30-12   Panelists and moderator log in; check technology

→ 12-12:15   Moderator welcomes audience; housekeeping items: how to engage, backup plan, Twitter hashtag, one-to two-minute introduction of panelists

→ 12:15-12:25   Audience poll; first round of questions and panel discussion

→ 12:25-12:35   Audience questions

→ 12:35-12:45   Second round of questions and panel discussion

→ 12:45-12:55   Audience questions

→ 12:55   Lightning-round answers from panelists

→ 1:00   Close

While I prefer to avoid sending panelists my questions prior to the event to maintain the spontaneity of answering in the moment, you may choose to send questions or even topic areas in advance.

VISIT ONLINE RESOURCES FOR:
An example of what a show-flow looks like.

TIP 4   HAVE A BACKUP PLAN FOR VIRTUAL PANELS

→ Ask everyone on the team to log in 30 minutes before the event to check all equipment.

→ Get telephone numbers for all panelists just in case you need to call them, for example, if the audio drops.

→ Send a group text to all panelists and any event producer, so you can readily communicate in the background, if needed.

→ Ask panelists to shut down all programs running on their computers to maximize bandwidth.

→ Provide a simple backup plan for the team if things go wrong (e.g., switch to Facebook live). (See Chapter 12 to read more about planning for the unexpected.)

TIP 5   START STRONG, END STRONG

Online audiences get bored quickly, so start with a short, interesting hook to grab everyone's attention. Plan how you will introduce yourself and welcome the audience; then mention the topical focus, panelists' names, and a bit about what the audience needs to know about the technology.

> Dispense with the long preamble, and get right into the discussion within one to two minutes so you don't lose the audience to multitasking.

TIP 6   KEEP IT MOVING

As a moderator, it's your job to keep the conversation moving. Tell panelists you want to keep comments to one to two minutes. In virtual panels, ask them to keep their eyes on the private communication channel you've established. This way, you can send them a private chat if they're talking too long, and be confident they'll see your note.

> If panelists run long in their comments, an easy place to interrupt is when they take a breath.

TIP 7   PRACTICE INCLUSION

Some audience members love to speak up and ask questions, and others don't. For those who prefer a less active role, give them the option to use Twitter or chat. For those who do speak up, thank them, call them by name, and acknowledge their contributions.

TIP 8   EXPAND DIVERSITY

As the panel moderator, you may not have any say in who your panelists are. If you do, ask yourself: "What point of view is missing from this panel?" Then seek out a diversity of voices. Diversity can relate to gender, age, race, ethnicity, religion, and/or geographical location. But it also comes from thinking, decision-making, or communication styles.

TIP 9   HYPERCONNECT WITH TWEETMEET

TweetMeets are custom chats where you use tools like Hootsuite or Tweetdeck to schedule text and images to appear as tweets during the event. This creates a social media conversation that amplifies the live discussion. You can even send your tweets to panelists prior to the event, so that they can also schedule their responses. This means that tweets appear at key moments during the discussion—giving the sense of a live discussion without having to manage it during the actual event. Organize your tweets into:

→ **Before:** Send tweets to market the event, introduce the panelists, and promote registration.

→ **During:** Invite panelists and audience members to tweet using the event hashtag. (Panelists can plan their tweets ahead of time based on a predetermined schedule.)

→ **After:** Share audience reactions, notable quotes from the discussion, and market follow-up events.

TIP 10   DELIGHT IN DISAGREEMENT

Whether your panel is live or virtual, disagreement is compelling because it's dramatic. It's even more imperative to find disagreement in virtual discussions to maintain attention. Tell your panelists you encourage healthy, lively debate, and agree on a process for how you'll wrap it up, so it doesn't get out of hand: a nudge in the chat or interrupting during a breath, for example.

And *practice!* For both moderators and panelists, practice until it looks like you've never done it before, whether that's alone or as a group. The more you practice, the freer you become to respond to what happens in the moment!

11.4	# How to Emcee an Event or Gathering (Online or Offline)

If you've been asked to emcee and you're not a professional, congratulations! It's a fun and fabulous opportunity to raise your visibility, showcase your personality, and connect with people.

The role of an emcee . . .

Do

→   Give the audience a smooth, fun, and connected experience.

- → Be the glue that holds the content, events, speakers, and audience together.

- → Cover and buy time amid delays.

- → Create an inclusive environment for all.

- → Create buzz and discussion among audience members.

Don't

- → Share your problems with the audience.

- → Apologize for shortcomings, real or imagined.

- → Get caught up in or distracted by hackers or hecklers.

- → Use off-color, sexist, racist, hurtful, or you-know-what-I'm-talking-about jokes or content.

- → Share inside jokes with the speakers and leave the audience in the dark.

STORY:
LADIES AND GENTLEMEN, OR GIRLS AND BOYS?

I once worked with a professional emcee who was a lovely person and a wonderful emcee. The opportunity: He was invited to emcee TEDxSeattle. The challenge: He was normally an emcee for children.

The TEDx audience is an intelligent group of adults who enjoy having their thinking challenged by amazing ideas. He said, "Everyone make an airplane sound. Now, open your arms wide like an airplane and turn to someone next to you with a 'whoosh' and hug them."

After listening to presentations on stem-cell heart transplants and how to bring about gender pay equity, the audience found his whimsical approach condescending. There wasn't anything wrong with his activity. It just didn't work for this event.

Assuming your style fits the gig, here's how to emcee like you were born for it:

TIP 1   KNOW YOUR AUDIENCE

Are they clients, customers, senior leaders, kids, co-workers, construction workers? Once you know the audience, consider how you need to show up—your strategic presence (Chapter 1). Tailor your messages and activities to their needs and interests.

TIP 2   DETERMINE WHAT KIND OF EXPERIENCE YOU WANT THEM TO HAVE

Energizing? Thoughtful? Fun? Challenging? Clarity about your goals will help determine the emotional tone you need to set.

TIP 3   HELP ALL SPEAKERS FEEL COMFORTABLE

If someone feels happy and comfortable before they walk out, chances are they will deliver with confidence. Aim to check on their comfort level before the event. Tell them what you're excited to hear about from them. And make sure you get their introduction down accurately.

TIP 4   BE THE COMPETENT PAIR OF HANDS

Providing answers and setting clear expectations are generous gifts for attendees navigating an event full of new content and experiences, so:

→   Educate the audience on how to use any technology they're being asked to engage with.

→   Communicate schedule changes, next steps, and important housekeeping notes.

→   Link sessions together by keeping track of key messages and emotions. Then summarize these for the audience as you tie them back to the event theme.

→   Preview coming attractions by saying, "Join us for our next event . . ."

→ Highlight the next thing people need to stick around for, or focus on an event at a specific time, "At 2:30 today . . ."

TIP 5 COORDINATE WITH THE COORDINATORS

Know the names and roles of the behind-the-scenes team, so if a snafu happens, you have the right support right away. Make sure you have a communication channel to the backstage team and feel comfortable using it in a pinch.

TIP 6 BUILD A GAME PLAN

If you're working with a professional events producer, they will likely provide a show-flow. If not, create your own, even if it's just high level: timings, content, people, visuals, music cues, and so on.

TIP 7 CREATE BUZZ

When asking the audience questions, pick questions that have opposing answers to enhance the discussion. "Are you a chocolate or vanilla person? Discuss."

TIP 8 REWARD ENGAGEMENT

Always thank the audience for their participation. Even better is if you can thank them for something specific: "I appreciate the insight that Shondra shared around connecting with their customers. As we've heard, that's not only crucial for customers, it's also crucial to our own sense of satisfaction. Thank you, Shondra."

By accepting invitations to take on different presentation roles—to being part of an ensemble—you can exponentially increase the reach of your message. And isn't that what speaking is all about?! Whether as a co-presenter, panelist, moderator, or emcee, say yes to opportunities to connect with more people in more ways. Stretching your comfort zone to expand your audience is worth it.

CHAPTER SUMMARY
KEY TAKEAWAYS:

- Moderating panels requires careful preparation, brevity, and inclusive language. Get in sync with co-presenters by identifying roles and rehearsing.

- Before accepting a role as a moderator or emcee, ask if your style is a good fit for the audience.

- New to emceeing? Lead with confidence by knowing and delivering on the event vibe, audience, tech, and show-flow.

The show must go on!

CHAPTER 12

When Things Go Wrong . . .

While I don't want to be a pessimist, snags *will* happen. They're just part of putting yourself out there. With great reward comes risk.

I once stepped out on stage to speak, and a light came loose from the ceiling, dropped on the stage, and nearly made me a goner. Another time, as I was speaking in a hotel ballroom, the pool on the level above started leaking through the ceiling. I didn't realize anything was wrong until I saw the people in the back re-enacting the *Titanic*. Yowser.

12.1 Tips to Keep Calm and Carry On

So here you are: You have 30 minutes to present, including Q&A, but you just lost 10 of it because the host has asked you to wait for some delayed audience members. As you attempt to begin, the folks in the meeting room next door start doing their rendition of *Braveheart* by pounding on the tables and shouting "Yes, YES, YEESSSSS!!!" Your participants start shouting, "We can't hear you!" You can't hear them either. What to do?

This actually happened to me once when I was presenting in Vegas. Here's what I did.

BREATHE

When we're stressed, we breathe too much. In fact, sometimes this fast over-breathing leads to hyperventilation. Instead of prepping your brain to flee by pumping it full of air, slow your breathing. Decreasing your breathing rate and volume will blunt the fight or flight system. One of the best ways to do this? Exhale. Breathe *out*. Blow it out like you're blowing through a straw.

> Have you ever watched athletes before a big moment? Just before the starting gun goes off? Notice what they do: They breathe *out* because a slow exhale helps them relax and calm the nervous system. It sends the message to the brain and body, "Don't worry, I got this."

CHOOSE YOUR STRESS: EUSTRESS OR DISTRESS?

Psychologists have studied what makes a peak performer like Serena Williams different from an average performer. How do peak performers sustain their performance over time, in many different situations?

Research shows that peak performers are able to maintain something called *eustress* as opposed to *distress*. Eustress happens when we are met with a challenge, but we believe we have the resources, skills, and talents to meet it. Under eustress, we lose track of time, become extremely focused, are highly creative, and can make effective, snap decisions in the moment. By contrast, distress paralyzes us.

TRUST YOUR TRAINING

The right time to teach our brains and bodies how to handle stress is *before* it happens. We do this by intentionally putting ourselves into stressful situations.

> The tools of improvisation are great for training our brains to respond quickly to unexpected issues.

By creating stressful simulations, you can help your brain become more flexible and adaptable—you can learn to think on your feet.

The crucial first step is learning to get comfortable with the uncertainty of the moment. Improv helps us learn this because it's *structured* uncertainty. We never know what's coming, but giving our brains structures, tools, and systems, we're able to respond with confidence.

So what did I do when "Braveheart" made an appearance in Vegas? I jumped up on the nearest table so that my voice could carry better over the room to the people in the back. Voilà! My audience could hear me, and we could carry on.

STORY:
LIFE GIVE YOU LEMONS?
IMPROVISE WITH AIR SWORDS

The wig flying off the head. The costume that falls off, leaving the wearer standing in underwear (or worse). The prop that was *supposed* to be on stage but has mysteriously gone missing. Every actor has an "Oh S***" story to tell. I once watched two students at Yale navigate what was meant to be a terrifying, deadly sword fight—without any swords. The weapons were supposed to have been hidden on stage. But the props master forgot to place them. So, they improvised with air swords. Did it change the moment? It sure did. Did it ruin the play? Not as much as it would have, had they run off stage to find their swords! The audience loved them for their hutzpah to forge ahead and improvise.

And for every horror story an actor tells about what went wrong, there's the corresponding tale of how well a gaff landed with the audience, how much the actor could feel the audience being fully on the edge *with* them. Most of all, actors talk about how much they sensed the audience rooting for them in those moments— and how thunderous applause broke out in honor of how they overcame what seemed insurmountable.

VISIT ONLINE RESOURCES FOR:
Improv exercises that help make your brain more flexible and adaptive in the moment by simulating stress.

12.2 Thinking Ahead, Virtually: Planning for the *Titanic*

Implementation intentions were created by psychologist Peter Gollwitzer in the 1990s to help people anticipate obstacles they might encounter when working to achieve a goal. They come in handy in the virtual world, where a lot can go wrong.

Studies conducted by Gollwitzer[12] showed that the use of implementation intentions can result in a higher probability of success, by helping our brains navigate life's curveballs by having a response ready. This "if/then" tool looks something like this: When I'm presenting tomorrow, if my sound goes out, then I will have my phone right next to me with the dial-in instructions so I can call into the presentation.

HOW TO PLAN FOR WHEN S*** HITS THE FAN

→ **Be specific.** Make an exhaustive list of everything you think could possibly go wrong. Then write down your specific response to each.

→ **Come up with at least two responses for every snafu.** Example: If I am presenting, and my kids burst into the room, then I will:

1. Smile and quickly introduce my kids to the audience, or

2. Calmly tell my audience we'll take a three-minute break, turn off my sound and video, and gently usher my kids out of the room.

> We can never anticipate *everything* that can go wrong. But capturing, in rehearsal, a list of things that *might* go wrong in performance means you'll prime the brain to easily manage any challenge— even those you didn't anticipate.

→ **Spend a few minutes each day working through potential issues.** You can visualize or walk through what you'll do when plans go awry. This will help you remember what to *actually* do in real time, if that crap *does* happen.

12.3	**Call in a Virtual Producer**

Give yourself the freedom and bandwidth to focus on your content and connections, *not* on the chat, by hiring a producer. This expert will manage all things technical. They can also keep an eye on audience needs and responses, so *you* can remain in concert with attendees.

> A producer is your safety net for when things go wrong so you can focus on what you do best.

12.4	**Embrace the Human**

Ultimately, we can't anticipate *everything* that will go wrong. There's the husband who walked into the room naked during his wife's presentation. The parrot who started shouting expletives in the team meeting. And the lawyer who couldn't get the cat filter off his face.

> Research shows that people warm to us when we show our vulnerability rather than hide it.

When we make a mistake, using a self-deprecating joke, "I'm having a senior moment," can endear us to the audience, create a connected moment of humor, or undermine our credibility. Three tips to self-deprecate, not self-sabotage:

1. **Tap the empathy.** Because most people fear public speaking, your audience is glad it's you up there, not them. Statements like, "Oh, you know that moment when your brain is running a marathon, but your mouth is doing a 5k?" will enlist your audience's empathy. They'll put themselves in your shoes, smile *with* you, and see you recover with grace and humor.

2. **Telegraph a snafu only when you need to.** If it's *huge*, call it out. If it's not, smile, breathe, and carry on. While you know your presentation backward and forward, your audience doesn't. Chances are, they won't even notice the *faux pas*.

3. **Prepare some frazzle phrases.** Don't wait for a glitch to think of a clever recovery. Memorize a few gracious first-aid phrases for the moment of frazzle.

After all, sometimes the "worst" mistakes equal the greatest gems—the keepers. Consider the snafus that stuck, like Dustin Hoffman's famous line from *Midnight Cowboy*: "I'm walkin' here!" The line wasn't in the movie and the taxi really did nearly hit him. Or Anthony Hopkins' erotic slurping sounds after his chianti, liver, and fava beans line in *The Silence of the Lambs*. He thought they were no longer filming and wanted to have fun with Jodie Foster by creeping her out.

> Presenting is inherently risky, on stage and on camera. Mistakes *will* happen. It's a performance—but not a movie. If you fumble a line, no one will yell, "CUT!" Mess up? Move on, and enjoy the ride.

As an actor, teacher, and coach, I've seen hundreds of great talks given by highly skilled and trained orators. But my favorite presentations, the ones I refer to over and over, have always been those given by people who loved their message more than the podium. For them, it wasn't about the act of speaking—it was about having something to say. No matter *what* happens with the audio or the lights or the Wi-Fi, return to your *message*—that's where the most important memories originate.

CHAPTER SUMMARY
KEY TAKEAWAYS:

- When snafus arise, breathe out and manage your thoughts to remain in eustress, the flip side of distress.

- Train your mind to be nimble and flexible when facing stress, so you *simulate* the stress, and learn from it.

- Have a plan for when the s*** hits the fan by preparing your responses to specific glitches and life's inevitable curveballs.

Gratitude

It takes a village, and sometimes an entire tribe, to help write a book. My tribe never let up on helping me push the boulder up and over the hill. Heartfelt gratitude goes out to my friend Andrea Driessen for sparking the idea, helping to keep it lit, and then meticulously editing many drafts. Also to my researcher Katy Anastasi and to editor extraordinaire, Shawn Finger, for her amazing work at helping me make my ideas and words leap off the page. My mom, Susan Farrington, for drinking margaritas with me and listening while I talked out each chapter before I wrote it. My other super-smart friend, Lisa Phelps Dawes, for reminding me to keep the end of the tunnel in sight. Rohit Bhargava and the Ideapress team for their endless patience. Dr. Frank Torok, who gave me my first job at Yale, and Dr. Roy Fluhrer for a lifetime of learning—mentors and sponsors are so important to have in life. My husband and our sweet furry family for their love and stress-reducing purrs, plays, and cuddles. (Okay, my husband doesn't exactly purr.) And to all my clients over the years who inspire me with their courage and willingness to experiment, learn, and grow.

Endnotes

1   Zandan, Noah, and Hallie Lynch, "Dress for the (Remote) Job You Want," *Harvard Business Review*, June 2020, https://hbr.org/2020/06/dress-for-the-remote-job-you-want.

2   Rizzolatti, Giacomo and Corrado Sinigaglia. *Mirrors in the Brain: How Our Minds Share Actions and Emotions*, Frances Anderson, tr. (New York: Oxford University Press, 2018).

3   Tannen, Deborah. "'Don't Just Sit There—Interrupt!' Pacing and Pausing in Conversational Style." *American Speech*, vol. 75 no. 4, 2000, pp. 393–395. *Project MUSE* muse.jhu.edu/article/2789.

4   https://www.t-kougei.ac.jp/activity/research/pdf/vol2-28-02.pdf

5   Baumeister, R. F., and M. R. Leary. (1995). "The need to belong: Desire for interpersonal attachments as a fundamental human motivation," *Psychological Bulletin* 117, 497–529.

6   Lai, Vicky. qtd. in University of Arizona, "How the brain finds meaning in metaphor," Science Daily, April 2, 2019, https://www.sciencedaily.com/releases/2019/04/190402113157.htm.

7   https://unwritten-record.blogs.archives.gov/2018/01/30/gettysburg-civil-war-monuments-nuclear-arsenals-and-dreams-of-peace/

8   SlideLizard, "The History and Evolution of PowerPoint," April 20, 2020, https://slidelizard.com/en/blog/powerpoint-history-and-versions.

9   Medina, John. *Brain Rules* (Seattle, WA: Pear Press, 2014).

10 Editorial Team, "How and Why to Use Visualization in Your Class," Wharton Interactive, April 2020, https://interactive.wharton.upenn.edu/learning-insights/how-and-why-use-visualization-your-class/; and Oppenheim, Lynn. *"A Study of the Effects of the Use of Overhead Transpar-*

encies on Business Meetings," (Philadelphia: Wharton Applied Research Center, 1981).

11 https://www.huffpost.com/entry/writing-by-hand-improves-your-memory-experts-say_n_61087608e4b0999d2084f66b https://www.the-learning-agency-lab.com/the-learning-curve/learn-better-through-writing/

12 Gollwitzer, Peter M. *Implementation Intentions: Strong Effects of Simple Plans* (Konstanz, Germany: Pear Press: 1999).

About the Author

Jacqueline Farrington has over 20 years' experience coaching leaders and their teams on how to use communications to inspire people and organizations to change. She blends her experience in the performing arts, vocal pedagogy, communications, psychology, and organizational/executive coaching to help her clients find unique communication solutions around challenges such as digital transformations, organizational culture change, the "Great Resignation," or engaging in conversations on social justice.

Her clients include multinationals such as Amazon and Microsoft, as well as start-ups and non-profits. She proudly served for many years as TEDx Seattle's Senior Speaker Coach, where she sourced, vetted, and prepared speakers for yearly sold-out audiences of 3,000. She was thrilled to see several speakers from that event move on to the global TED stage. In addition to her time teaching at Yale, she has lectured and taught at the London Business School, Rutgers University, Imperial College, and other institutions.

She and her husband are currently working on their next project: a small organic family farm and farm-to-table events space.

Index

Want help with your next high-stakes communication challenge?

Let us help you up your presentation game.

→ Get help writing a speech or presentation

→ Learn how to deliver a presentation that captures and holds the audience's attention

→ Manage "the nerves" before, during, and even after your presentation

→ Design compelling (not boring) presentation visuals

→ Improve your connection with your audience

LEARN MORE:
farringtonpartners.com